Ninja Foodi

Cookbook for Beginners

Simple, Easy and Delicious 5 Ingredients Ninja Foodi
Recipes for Fast and Healthy Meals

By Angela Taylor

Table of Content

Introduction..1

  From My Kitchen to Your Tummy...3

  Understanding the Make of the Ninja Foodi...5

  Pressure Cooking..7

  Air Frying...8

Breakfast and Brunch Recipes...10

  Raspberry-Peanut Butter Oatmeal..10

  Kale-Barley Breakfast Bowl...11

  Raisin-Coconut Rye Porridge..12

  Herby Eggs in Avocados...13

  Collard-Asparagus Baked Eggs..14

  Mushroom & Goat Cheese Oatmeal...15

  Mushroom Frittata..16

  Egg Caprese Brunch Cups..17

  Chicken Brunch Burritos..18

  Menemen (Turkish Baked Eggs)..19

Snacks, Appetizers, and Sides Recipe...20

  Blueberry-Nutella Bites..20

  Churro Bites..21

  Barbecued Beef Meatballs..22

  Bacon Jalapeño Poppers...23

  Creamy Cilantro Polenta...24

  Sweet Butter Carrots...25

  Spicy Feta Potatoes...26

  Cheesy Vegetable Rice..27

  Mexican-Style Rice and Beans...28

  Tangy Steamed Veggies..29

Desserts Recipe..30

  Tapioca Pudding...30

  New York Style Cheesecake...31

  Yellow Cake Pineapple Upside Down..32

Raspberry Cheesecake...33

Caramel Popcorns..34

Chocolate Crème de Pot...35

Apricots Dulche de Leche...36

Blackberry Cobbler..37

Mango Rice Pudding..38

Baked Stuffed Apples..39

Fish and Seafood Recipe..40

Rustic Seafood Pot..40

Spicy Fried Salmon with Avocado Salsa...41

Shrimp Bisque...42

Fried Scallops in Cilantro Sauce...43

Breaded Trout with Parsley Pesto...44

Paprika Tuna Cakes..45

Red Wine Poached Salmon...46

Garlic Lemon Shrimp with Asparagus...47

Tuna in Mango Sauce...48

Mussel Stew with Red Wine...49

Poultry Recipe..50

Pomegranate Chicken Tagine..50

Adobo Drumsticks..51

Paprika Thighs with Summer Vegetables...52

Mushroom and Chicken Cacciatore...53

Thai Chicken Curry Rice...54

Chili-Mango Glazed Chicken..55

Sesame Orange Chicken...56

Balsamic-Rosemary Whole Chicken...57

Chicken Parmigiana..58

Thai Sweet Chili Chicken..59

Beef, Lamb, and Pork Recipe..60

Short Ribs with Tomato-Fig Chutney...60

Beef Meatballs in Honey-Orange Sauce...62

Spicy Beef Pitas..64

Lamb Macaroni Casserole..65

Lamb, Mushroom, and Rice Mix..66

Lamb Rogan Josh..67

Lemon Pork Chops with Sriracha...69

Pork Prosciutto and Corn Masala...70

Rosemary Lemon Pork Chops...71

Tuscan Pork Chops..72

Vegan, Vegetarian, and Vegetables Recipe..**73**

Vegan Vegetable Minestrone...73

Vegetable Tart..74

Pappardelle with Tomatoes and Arugula..75

Tofu Taco Quinoa Bowls...76

Creamy Cheesy Fettucine..77

Moroccan Chickpea Curry...78

Yellow Lentil Dhal with Spinach..79

Roasted Broccoli-Mushroom Plate with Almonds...80

Tangy Green Beans with Peanuts..81

Steamed Cabbage Wedges with Chili Lemon Dressing......................................82

Rice, Grains, and Pasta Recipe..**83**

Herby Chicken Rice...83

Thai Teriyaki Rice...84

Italian Beef Cheesy Rice...85

Corn & Scallion Oatmeal..86

Barley-Spinach Bowl...87

Raisins Buckwheat Pilaf..88

Creole-Style Grits & Shrimp...89

Watercress Tagliatelle with Smoked Salmon..91

Creamy Bucatini with Chicken...92

Spaghetti in Saffron Sauce..93

Introduction

Hey there!

I'm happy about your purchase! I'm thankful for the opportunity to share this cookbook with you!

I am a busy mom-entrepreneur and one of my venture duties is to organize conferences and coach many business people on essential business development practices. As I share my business experiences with others, I also love to share my food and lifestyle experiences too. Hence, I wrote this cookbook to share one of those moments with you.

So yes! I love bagging the numbers while on business, but when it comes to pleasure, nothing does me well, like a good cook from my kitchen –also, a no-contact vacation with so much ocean closeness and fresh seafood.

My kitchen moments with my children are ones that I can't exhaust, and so I am happy about my recent culinary documentation of these experiences. I share them with you, and I hope you have a good time traveling through them.

Count me a pro on stir-fries, baked foods, desserts, and fried chicken! Unfortunately, I lost this touch about two years ago, as life became more real while combining a hectic schedule with lengthy cooking processes. What was once a collection of happy dinner moments to look forward to ended up being one of my most bizarre parts of the day. The thought of my tiresome stovetop alone on my way home from the grind dropped my adrenaline in an instant. And so, I sort to many takeouts for the family, which we both know can be unhealthy.

Although the experience, I won't miss an opportunity to thank my Granny, who stood in the gap many times during these periods. She prepped my family sumptuous, homemade, American cuisines to keep the love ablaze in my home. And by her, I learned about the Ninja Foodi. No wonder her chicken pieces were always super crispy!

Fast forward, it's been eleven months since I began using the Ninja Foodi, and I couldn't be grateful enough to the manufacturers for the light shone on my culinary life. I've been back to cooking, and I am pumped on the cook; thanks to this device!

If you are a busy person, a lazy cook, a bachelor, or merely a tech-savvy individual that is crazy about kitchen appliances too, this cookbook is for you.

In this book, my goal is to simplify the process of cooking to the least possible while assuming that everyone out there is as busy as I am. Therefore, I compiled my love for the Ninja Foodi into eighty tasty, self-developed recipes that will rock your cooking life for the better. Even more, the book aims at providing recipes that use not more than five main ingredients per cook to quicken the kitchen time spent. Hence, making the book ideal for singles, students and minimalist cooks.

And if you thought that the reduction in ingredients list wouldn't make the foods delicious, you should be heading over to your first recipe already!

While I am in haste to get you cooking already, I'll have you join me on the next pages as we dig into the Ninja Foodi and the good stuff that I have for you.

Cheers to many days of quick and moreish cooking!

From My Kitchen to Your Tummy

You see, after I used my Ninja Foodi for a while, I sort to starting a side business where I would supply these devices to restaurants and homes at a profit. And so, I spoke to one of my closest friends and business associates, who surprisingly turned down my idea.

Why? Because she was skeptical about the long-term effect that appliances like this may have on our health. How archaic and absurd?

You see, so long were the days when our great grandmothers spent a decent amount of time in kitchens prepping foods for the families as a chore that never ended. And so, to have a mindset about such ideologies, I reckon you to realize that we live in an advanced world. Therefore, if you have this mentality, I encourage that you drop it before moving further on the read.

Long cooking times and processes are far-fetched in recent styles of cooking; hence, it is an excellent place to embrace devices like the Ninja Foodi in our kitchens.

From the business side of things, I believe every second is an essential dollar and should offer good value to whatever that it is applied. And while I have my sentiments against the stovetop, I know the world is in the right place with devices that do not only simplify cooking but create fun moments while cooking. The Ninja Foodi is one!

And if you are still skeptical about the safety of these devices; hence, you will stick to old, hectic ways of cooking, I dedicate this paragraph to say that *"it is safe and wise."*

Enough of the long talk ☺

Now to me and why I wrote this cookbook?

In its simplicity, I love to cook and I love to cook the fastest, and easiest!

This cookbook is an assemblage of my idea to use ingredients that are easily accessible to us while limiting the count to a few for making lip-smacking foods. I restrict the ingredients in these recipes to at most five mains per recipe while supporting this team of players with foods that you (may) already have in your pantry.

I share recipes covering breakfast, brunch, lunch, dinner, vegan & vegetarian, desserts, snacks, and a wide range of meat options. While I would have loved to load the book with many more recipes that I have made with the Ninja Foodi, space and time would only allow me to share eighty of them. But these are bangers! And trust me, you're going to be screaming at the excellent outcomes and tastes that you make out of them.

My hope with this cookbook being one of many more to come is to improve your culinary lifestyle with delicacies that you will look forward to making. A compilation of classics that will redirect your focus from unhealthy eating to moments of joy shared with loved ones coming from your kitchen.

One thing holds, all the foods shared here have been thoroughly tested, tried, and enjoyed by many mouths to ensure that they are treats once landed on your plates.

I hope to be cooking with you for many days to come and even with your grandchildren.

Enjoy the exposé to a world of tender, crispy, crunchy, fast, and mouthwatering foods while you share these with many.

Have a good time cooking!

Understanding the Make of the Ninja Foodi

What constitutes the petite embodiment of this device? Well, I must warn you that it is heavier than it looks, so don't downplay its sight for light-weight.

The Ninja Foodi blends the best of two worlds in its unique self; pressure cooking and air frying. Meaning, while two separate devices will get you the goal of pressure cooking foods and air frying with little oil, the Ninja Foodi offers these feature on a better platter. All in one with more!

Best known to be a combo of the pressure cooker and the air fryer, the Ninja Foodi offers other functions that allow you to Bake, Roast, Steam, Slow-cook, Sear, Sauté, and Broil with the aid of two lids and accompanying accessories.

Think of crispy chicken with fries, Thai curries, a range of cheesecakes and the opportunity to make tasty snacks on end. This single device gets you all of these in perfection. Salivating mouth already? Wait until you try the recipes!

Lid One: The Air Crisping Lid

This lid is a constant attachment to the Foodi that opens to the side of the pot and is used for air frying, baking, roasting, or broiling foods. It stands as the bulkier of the two lids but performs crisping magic like none other.

While I will love that this lid was detachable, it doesn't break a leg to have it sitting by the pot while pressure cooking. I bet that you can deal with its constant presence too!

Lid Two: The Pressure Cooking Lid

Being a removable lid, this allows for tenderizing foods to the best. I mean meat falling off the bones without any hassle.

Thinking of making soups, steamed foods, rice, stews, etc., you should make them using the pressure cooking approach with the aid of the lid. Trust me, the technique of applying pressure on foods during this process results in the softest and tastiest of foods than a stovetop or regular oven will offer.

How About Combining Both Functions For Meal Prep?

Oh yes! This option is well embraced when using the Ninja Foodi, and in the recipe collection, you will find recipes that allow you tenderize foods with the pressure cooker while enabling you to crisp these foods to the best of crunch, as you desire.

My favorite makes are short ribs and pork ribs in this case. I will usually cook the seasoned meat over a cup of water, set in the inner pot on the rack until tender and then have them browned with the Air Crisping function for the best result.

In my opinion, I believe trying out foods that allow you to use both functions at once on recipes, enable you to utilize the Foodi to its best.

Let's Look At The Other Offerings That You Get With The Foodi?

As mentioned earlier, the Ninja Foodi allows Steaming, Slow Cooking, Searing/Sautéing, Baking, Roasting, and Broiling.

Once you've purchased the device, an accompanying set of accessories are provided to aid with cooking. These are:

-**A Non-Stick Pot:** a removable and replaceable pot that must be placed on the base always before cooking in any form. It accommodates at least four servings per cook and offers a direct cook within the pot. Meanwhile, it is easy on the clean too. I purchased one more of this pot to aid with cooking more portions when I do not want to transfer the food in one, clean quickly and continue cooking. This convenience helps when I host friends and family –it aids with a smooth cook.

-**A Reversible Rack:** acting as a trivet like other pressure cookers may have. Position this rack in the inner pot in a lower or upper position over at least half a cup of water to initiate the cook. Foods should be placed on the rack for steaming, baking, or air frying.

-**A Cook & Crisp Basket:** for most dishes that require the use of the air frying techniques, placing food in this unit is an excellent way to get your meals cooked to perfection.

Meanwhile, for the flexibility to cook foods in a wider range like making bundt cakes, the Foodi makes provision to use other accessories not included in the initial package when the device is bought. You may purchase these accessories from stores like Amazon; however, they should be Ninja certified.

How To Use The Ninja Foodi?

1. Preheating: It is crucial to preheat the inner pot of the Foodi before introducing food to the device. It takes the approach of regular cooking on the stovetop or oven where preheating is essential to prepare the oven or pot for a good cook. Make sure to preheat the inner pot for at least 5 minutes before adding food.

2. Water For Pressure-Cooking: pressure-cooking requires steam to do its work, and some form of liquid activates this process. Therefore, ensure to add at least half a cup of water to the inner pot before pressure cooking foods to drive your cook to success.

3. The Lids: The Ninja Foodi includes two necessary lids, the Air Crisping Lid for air frying and the Pressure Lid for pressure-cooking. Make good use of the lids as directed by the recipe at hand. I elaborated on the lids above this write-up. Check it out if you skipped it.

4. Using The Inner Pot Always: interestingly, the Foodi detects an override if the inner pot isn't inserted before a cook. It is smart! Hence, make sure to keep the inner pot locked in always before performing any of the pressure-cooking or air frying functions.

Pressure Cooking

SEAR / SAUTE: Apply this function to preheat the pot, for searing, stir-frying, or sautéing foods. To use, turn on the Ninja Foodi and select the Sear/ Sauté function; adjust the temperature between Low and High as preferred. To preheat, set the timer to 5 minutes before beginning the cook as the recipe guides.

PRESSURE: For all foods that require pressure-cooking, use this function. To enable, include at least a half cup of liquid in the inner pot, add the food (either directly to the pot or placed on the rack) and close the Pressure Lid on the pot. Also, lock the Vent nozzle in the Seal position and adjust the temperature between Low and High. Set the time according to the recipe's requirements and press Start/Stop to begin cooking.

STEAM: Activate this function for steaming vegetables, seafood, and meats. Make sure to add at least one (1) cup of liquid to the inner pot, fix in the Reversible Rack in the lower or upper position, and place your food on top. After, lock the Pressure lid in place and then the Vent in the Seal position. Press Start/Stop to begin steaming.

SLOW COOKER: How awesome that slow-cooking is allowed on the Ninja Foodi! Prepare broth, soups, etc. using this function for excellent results, as other slow cookers will offer. To apply, add food with at least one (1) cup of liquid to the inner pot and close the Pressure Lid in place. Make sure to lock the Vent nozzle in the Seal position. Adjust the temperature setting between (High – 4 hours to 8 hours) and (Low -6 hours to 8 hours). Press Start/Stop to begin slow cooking.

VENT: The Vent is a nozzle on top of the Pressure lid to be always locked when pressure-cooking. By keeping the vent locked, steam retains in the pot and aids in cooking foods to perfection. After each pressure-cook, the vent should first be released to let out all the steam in the pot before opening the Pressure Lid. Always ensure to wear a protective glove before opening the vent after cooking to prevent burns.

Air Frying

AIR CRISP: Consider the Air Crisp function when air frying foods. Like you would have fried chicken in a pot of hot oil on a stovetop, this function takes off that extra work. Meanwhile, it gives you crunchier results by circulating hot air over slightly greased foods. To enable, place the Reversible Rack or Cook or Crisp basket in the inner pot. Close the Air Crisp lid, adjust the temperature as required by the recipe and set the time to 5 minutes. Press Start/Stop to preheat the lid.

To cook, open the lid, add your prepared food to the rack or basket and close the lid. Adjust the temperature and time setting according to the recipe's request. Press Start/Stop to begin air crisping.

BAKE/ ROAST: In the same manner as the Air Crisping function, the Ninja Foodi allows for baking and roasting within the unit. Before baking or roasting, preheat the Air Crisp lid as you would for air crisping and introduce food to the pot in the same way. However, the function to use in this case will be Bake/Roast.

BROIL: And the same approach works for broiling too. Preheat the lid in the same manner as you would Air Crisp and cook foods in a similar direction as the recipe requires using the Broil function.

My Final Verdict

Should I be saying more after this much elaboration about the Ninja Foodi? If you are contemplating taking on this journey into easy and fun cooking with me, you shouldn't. Head over online and make a purchase.

My reasons?

The Ninja Foodi combines the better of two worlds: pressure-cooking and air frying but more actually. I find it to be that single appliance that takes care of the duty of a stovetop, an oven, a pressure cooker, an air fryer, a grill, and a searing torch. Imagine having a kitchen space scattered with these devices. Such a mess it will be, I believe! So, here, multi-functionality is achieved.

It is less expensive when compared to the amount of money that will be spent on purchasing these different appliances for different uses. And to make things even better, this dude saves you so much counter space to make your kitchen look minimalist. This advantage offers you the extra space to prep foods.

Meanwhile, for its petite look, the Ninja Foodi is weighty; hence, moving it about may not be wise. You, however, can carry it along for outdoor parties once you have a power source to connect. How awesome did outdoor parties get?

And talking of power, going this route is a better option to save on electricity and gas. In a place where the world is crying out for saving, purchasing the Ninja Foodi is an excellent way to contribute your quota to making the world a better place.

I should have convinced you by now. I'm happy to see you ready and set to begin cooking these sumptuous meals. Some of my favorites being the fruit-infused delicacies and the decadent collection of desserts.

Meanwhile, the recipes are flexible enough to be altered on ingredients. Feel at ease to swap ingredients to fit your diet and supply availability. Although, ensure that the components exchanged are direct alternatives. I wouldn't want you making disappointing dishes!

I'll leave things here now and wish you a happy time exploring the Ninja Foodi and working with few ingredients. Make sure to try out the more straightforward recipes and work your way up to the harder ones for skill perfection. Meanwhile, do share your foods with others and watch them get impressed by your master skill.

I will head on now to my next project and hope to share that with you soon.

Cheers again to the many days of enjoyable cooking!

Breakfast and Brunch Recipes

Raspberry-Peanut Butter Oatmeal

Prep time: 5 minutes | Cook time: 13 minutes | Serves: 4

Ingredients:

5-Ingredients:

1 cup old-fashioned rolled oats

2 cups whole milk

2 tbsp raspberry jam

3 tbsp peanut butter

¼ cup fresh raspberries to serve

Instructions

1. Turn on the Ninja Foodi and adjust to Medium heat.
2. Pour the oats, milk, jam, and peanut butter into the inner pot and mix well.
3. Close the Pressure Lid and lock the vent to Seal. Set the temperature to High and set the time to 3 minutes. Press Start to begin cooking.
4. After cooking, perform a natural pressure release for 10 minutes, then a quick pressure release to let out the remaining steam. Open the lid.
5. Spoon the food into serving bowls and top with the raspberries. Serve warm.

Nutrition Facts per Serving

Calories 214 | Fats 7.6g | Carbs 37.25g | Net Carbs 32.85 | Protein 27.44g

Kale-Barley Breakfast Bowl

Prep time: 10 minutes | Cook time: 30 minutes | Serves: 4

Ingredients:

5-Ingredients:

1 cup pearl barley

4 oz baby kale, chopped

¼ cup finely chopped red onion

2 scallions, chopped for garnishing

4 oz ham, chopped

Items from your pantry:

1 tbsp olive oil

2 cups chicken broth

Salt and freshly ground black pepper to taste

¼ tsp red chili flakes

Instructions

1. Select Sear/Sauté mode, adjust to Medium High, and choose Start/Stop to preheat the pot for 5 minutes.
2. Heat the olive oil in the inner pot and sauté the barley and onion until fragrant, 5 minutes.
3. Mix in the chicken broth and season with salt and black pepper.
4. Cover with the Pressure Lid and lock the vent to Seal. Select Pressure, set to High, and the time to 18 minutes. Press Start to begin cooking.
5. After cooking, perform a quick pressure release to let out the steam, and open the lid.
6. Stir in the ham, kale, and allow the kale to wilt for 2 minutes. Adjust the taste with salt and black pepper.
7. Dish the food into serving bowls, garnish with the scallions and red chili flakes.
8. Serve warm.

Nutrition Facts per Serving

Calories 436 | Fats 14.63g | Carbs 42.86g | Net Carbs 33.86g | Protein 33.61g

Raisin-Coconut Rye Porridge

Prep time: 15 minutes | Cook time: 5 minutes | Serves: 4

Ingredients:

5-Ingredients:

1 cup rye flakes

1 ¼ cups coconut milk

2 tbsp maple syrup

¾ cup raisins

2 tbsp coconut flakes for garnishing

Items from your pantry:

A pinch of salt

1 cup water

1 tsp vanilla extract

Instructions

1. In the inner pot, add all the ingredients and mix well.
2. Cover with the Pressure Lid and lock the vent to Seal. Choose Pressure, set to High, the timer to 5 minutes, and press Start/Stop to begin cooking.
3. After cooking, perform a natural pressure release for 10 minutes, then a quick pressure release, and open the lid.
4. Stir and dish the porridge. Top with the coconut flakes and serve warm.

Nutrition Facts per Serving

Calories 303 | Fats 19.02g | Carbs 31.68g | Net Carbs 26.78g | Protein 4.58g

Herby Eggs in Avocados

Prep time: 10 minutes | Cook time: 4 minutes | Serves: 4

Ingredients:

5-Ingredients:

2 large ripe avocados, halved and pitted

4 large eggs, cracked into a bowl

½ cup grated cheddar cheese

1 tbsp freshly chopped parsley to garnish

1 tbsp freshly chopped scallions to garnish

Items from your pantry:

Salt and freshly ground black pepper to taste

1 ½ tsp dried Italian herb mix

Instructions

1. Pour 1 cup of water into the inner pot and fix in the Reversible Rack in the lower position.
2. Spoon out half of the avocado flesh in each piece and fill each with one egg; season with the salt, black pepper, herb mix, and cheddar cheese. Carefully place the filled avocados on the rack.
3. Cover with the Pressure Lid and lock the vent to Seal. Select Pressure, adjust to High, and set the timer to 4 minutes. Press Start/Stop to begin cooking.
4. After cooking, perform a quick pressure release to let out all the steam, and open the lid.
5. Use tongs to remove the avocados carefully and transfer to serving plates.
6. Garnish with the parsley, scallions, and serve afterward.

Nutrition Facts per Serving

Calories 184 | Fats 11.12g | Carbs 8.67g | Net Carbs 8.47g | Protein 12.3g

Collard-Asparagus Baked Eggs

Prep time: 10 minutes | Cook time: 3 minutes | Serves: 4

Ingredients:

5-Ingredients:

½ cup finely chopped broccoli

½ cup chopped asparagus

½ cup chopped Swiss collards

4 large eggs

¼ cup crumbled ricotta cheese

Items from your pantry:

½ tsp onion powder

½ tsp garlic powder

Salt and freshly ground black pepper to taste

Instructions

1. Pour 1 cup of water into the inner pot and fix in the Reversible Rack in the lower position.
2. Grease 4 medium ramekins with cooking spray and create layers of the ingredients in this manner: broccoli, asparagus, and collards. Season with the onion powder, garlic powder, and create a hole in the center of the greens.
3. Pour an egg into each ramekin hole and top with the ricotta cheese, salt, and black pepper.
4. Cover with the Pressure Lid and lock the vent to Seal. Select Pressure; adjust to High, and set the cook time to 2 minutes. Press Start to begin steaming.
5. After cooking, perform a quick pressure release, and open the lid. Carefully remove the ramekins onto a flat surface.
6. Allow cooling for 1 minute and serve afterward.

Nutrition Facts per Serving

Calories 90 | Fats 6.6g | Carbs 2.65g | Net Carbs 1.95g | Protein 5.2g

Mushroom & Goat Cheese Oatmeal

Prep time: 10 minutes | Cook time: 10 minutes | Serves: 4

Ingredients:

5-Ingredients:

1 cup sliced baby bella mushrooms

1 tsp fresh rosemary leaves

1 cup chopped baby spinach

1 cup old fashioned rolled oats

¼ cup crumbled goat cheese

Items from your pantry:

1 tbsp butter

1 garlic clove, minced

Salt and freshly ground black pepper to taste

2 cups vegetable broth

¼ tsp red chili flakes

Instructions

1. Select Sear/Sauté mode, adjust to Medium, and choose Start/Stop to preheat the pot for 5 minutes.
2. Melt the butter in the inner pot and sauté the mushrooms until softened, 5 minutes. Mix in the garlic and rosemary; cook until fragrant, 1 minute. Season with salt and black pepper.
3. Stir in the spinach to wilt and then, the oats, vegetable broth, and red chili flakes.
4. Cover with the Pressure Lid and lock the vent to Seal. Select Pressure, set to High, and the time to 3 minutes. Press Start.
5. After cooking, perform a natural pressure release for 10 minutes, then a quick pressure release to let out the remaining steam, and open the lid.
6. Stir the food and adjust the taste with salt and black pepper.
7. Spoon the oatmeal into serving bowls and top with the goat cheese. Serve warm.

Nutrition Facts per Serving

Calories 1252 | Fats 131.64g | Carbs 16.73g | Net Carbs 12.83 | Protein 17.01g

Mushroom Frittata

Prep time: 15 minutes | Cook time: 20 minutes | Serves: 4

Ingredients:

5-Ingredients:

1 cup sliced mixed mushrooms

8 large eggs

½ cup heavy cream

1 tsp fresh thyme leaves

1 cup shredded Gruyere cheese

Items from your pantry:

2 tbsp butter

1 medium white onion, chopped

Salt and freshly ground black pepper to taste

Instructions

1. Select Sear/Sauté mode, adjust to Medium, and choose Start/Stop to preheat the pot for 5 minutes.
2. Melt the butter in the inner pot and sauté the bell pepper, onion, and mushrooms until softened, 5 minutes.
3. Meanwhile, in a medium bowl, whisk the eggs with salt, black pepper, and allow sitting for 1 minute. Whisk in the heavy cream, thyme, and half of the Gruyere cheese.
4. Pour the egg mixture over the vegetables and stir to distribute the eggs evenly. Allow cooking (undisturbed) until the edges are set, 7 to 9 minutes. Pierce any bubbles that form using the spatula to let out air from the frittata.
5. Press Stop to cancel the Sear/Sauté function and run the spatula in and around the edges of the frittata.
6. Close the Air Crisping Lid; choose Bake/Roast and set the temperature to 375°F, and time to 3 minutes. Press Start to begin baking.
7. After 1 minute, open the lid and sprinkle the remaining cheese on the frittata. Close the lid and cook for the remaining 2 minutes.
8. Once the timer ends, carefully open the lid and rest the frittata for 2 minutes.
9. Slice into wedges and serve.

Nutrition Facts per Serving

Calories 349 | Fats 32.64g | Carbs 1.45g | Net Carbs 1.45g | Protein 24.33g

Egg Caprese Brunch Cups

Prep time: 10 minutes | Cook time: 5 minutes |Serves: 4

Ingredients:

5-Ingredients:

4 thin slices ham

4 tbsp shredded mozzarella cheese

4 cherry tomatoes, halved

1 tbsp freshly chopped basil leaves

Items from your pantry:

Salt and freshly ground black pepper to taste

Instructions

1. Pour 1 cup of water into the inner pot and fix in the Reversible Rack in the lower position.
2. Line 4 medium ramekins with one ham each, crack an egg each per ramekin, and top with the mozzarella cheese, tomatoes, basil, salt, and black pepper. Cover the ramekins with foil.
3. Cover with the Pressure Lid and lock the vent to Seal. Select Pressure, adjust to High and set the timer to 3 minutes. Press Start to continue cooking.
4. Once done cooking, perform a quick pressure release and carefully open the lid.
5. Use tongs to remove the ramekins onto a flat surface. Take off the foil and allow cooling for 1 minute.
6. Serve warm afterward.

Nutrition Facts per Serving

Calories 68 | Fats 4.02g | Carbs 1.56g | Net Carbs 1.56g | Protein 6.39g

Chicken Brunch Burritos

Prep time: 10 minutes | Cook time: 26 minutes | Serves: 4

Ingredients:

5-Ingredients:

1 lb. ground chicken

1 medium red bell pepper, deseeded and diced

½ cup black beans, rinsed and drained

3 whole-wheat tortillas

¾ cup grated Monterey Jack cheese

Items from your pantry:

1 medium yellow onion, diced

1 tsp onion powder

1 tsp garlic powder

Salt and freshly ground black pepper to taste

½ cup chicken broth

Instructions

1. In the inner pot, add the chicken, onion powder, garlic powder, salt, black pepper, bell pepper, onion, beans, and chicken broth.
2. Cover with the Pressure Lid and lock the vent to Seal. Select Pressure, adjust to High and set the timer to 11 minutes. Press Start to cook.
3. After cooking, perform a natural pressure release for 10 minutes, then a quick pressure release to let out the remaining steam and open the lid.
4. Stir and adjust the taste with salt and black pepper.
5. Select Sear/Sauté mode, adjust to Medium, and choose Start/Stop to cook the food further until the liquid reduces by half and the filling thickens, 5 minutes.
6. Lay the tortilla wraps on a clean, flat surface, spoon the food onto the wraps and top with the cheese. Roll and slice the wraps into halves.
7. Serve immediately.

Nutrition Facts per Serving

Calories 145 | Fats 4.6g | Carbs 24.15g | Net Carbs 22.85g | Protein 2.63g

Menemen (Turkish Baked Eggs)

Prep time: 10 minutes | Cook time: 9 minutes | Serves: 4

Ingredients:

5-Ingredients:

1 red bell pepper, deseeded and chopped

1 green bell pepper, deseeded and chopped

2 cups chopped tomatoes

4 large eggs, crack into a bowl

2 tbsp freshly chopped mint leaves

Items from your pantry:

2 tbsp olive oil

1 onion, finely chopped

4 garlic cloves, minced

Salt and freshly ground black pepper to taste

Instructions

1. Select Sear/Sauté mode, adjust to Medium, and choose Start/Stop to preheat the pot for 5 minutes.
2. Heat olive oil in the inner pot and sauté the onion and bell pepper until softened, 5 minutes. Stir in the garlic and cook until fragrant, 30 seconds.
3. Mix in the tomatoes and cook until slightly softened for 5 minutes.
4. Create 4 holes in the sauce and pour into each hole an egg. Season with salt and black pepper.
5. Cover with the Pressure Lid and lock the vent to Seal. Select Pressure, adjust to High and set the timer to 3 minutes. Press Start to bake.
6. After cooking, perform a quick pressure release to let out all the steam and carefully open the lid.
7. Dish the food onto serving plates and garnish with the mint leaves.

Nutrition Facts per Serving

Calories 37 | Fats 2.02g | Carbs 1.54g | Net Carbs 1.44g | Protein 3.29g

Snacks, Appetizers, and Sides Recipe

Blueberry-Nutella Bites

Prep time: 10 minutes | Cook time: 12 minutes | Chilling time: 30 minutes | Serves: 4

Ingredients:

3-Ingredients:

2 large eggs

1 cup Nutella

14 fresh blueberries

Item from your pantry:

¼ cup plain flour

Instructions

1. In a medium bowl, whisk the eggs and Nutella until smoothly combined. Mix in the flour well.
2. Grease a silicone egg bite tray with cooking spray and fill halfway with the Nutella mixture. Drop two blueberries into each hole and cover with the rest of the Nutella mixture. Wrap the muffin tray with foil.
3. Pour 1 cup of water in the inner pot, fix in the Reversible Rack, and place the egg tray bite on the rack.
4. Close the Air Crisping Lid. Choose Bake/Roast; adjust the temperature to 375°F and the timer to 12 minutes. Press Start to begin baking.
5. After, open the lid and carefully remove the egg tray.
6. Take off the foil, allow cooling, and transfer the tray to a refrigerator. Chill for 30 minutes.
7. Serve after as snacks.

Nutrition Facts per Serving

Calories 158| Fats 10.77g | Carbs 5.34g | Net Carbs 5.34g | Protein 10.77g

Churro Bites

Prep time: 10 minutes | Cook time: 12 minutes | Chilling time: 30 minutes | Serves: 4

Ingredients:

4-Ingredients:

1 (21 oz) box cinnamon swirl crumb cake & muffin mix

1 brown sugar packet (included in cake mix box)

1 cup heavy cream

2 eggs

Items from your pantry:

1 tsp cinnamon powder

4 tbsp brown sugar

1 tbsp granulated sugar

Instructions

1. In a medium bowl, mix the muffin mix, brown sugar mix, heavy cream, eggs, ½ tsp of the cinnamon powder, and brown sugar until smoothly combined.
2. Grease a silicone egg bite tray with cooking spray and fill halfway with the cinnamon mixture. Cover the muffin tray with foil afterward.
3. Pour 1 cup of water in the inner pot, fix in the Reversible Rack, and place the egg tray bite on the rack.
4. Close the Air Crisping Lid. Choose Bake/Roast; adjust the temperature to 375°F and the timer to 12 minutes. Press Start to begin baking.
5. After, open the lid and carefully remove the egg tray.
6. Take off the foil, allow cooling, and transfer the tray to a refrigerator. Chill for 30 minutes.
7. To serve: in a plate mix the remaining cinnamon powder with the sugar. Pop the snacks out of the egg tray and roll in the sugar-cinnamon mix until well coated.
8. Enjoy after as snacks.

Nutrition Facts per Serving

Calories 828 | Fats 31.08g | Carbs 128g | Net Carbs 125g | Protein 10.56g

Barbecued Beef Meatballs

Prep time: 10 minutes | Cook time: 10 minutes | Serves: 4

Ingredients:

3-Ingredients:

1 cup honey

2 cups BBQ sauce

1 lb. frozen beef meatballs

Item from your pantry:

½ cup chicken broth

Instructions

1. In the inner pot, mix the honey, BBQ sauce, and chicken broth. Arrange the meatballs in the sauce and spoon the sauce to coat the meat well.
2. Cover with the Pressure Lid and lock the vent to Seal. Select Pressure, adjust to High and set the timer to 5 minutes. Press Start to begin cooking.
3. After cooking, perform a quick pressure release to let out all the steam and carefully open the lid.
4. Using a slotted spoon, remove the meatballs onto a serving plate, insert toothpicks, and serve as appetizers.

Nutrition Facts per Serving

Calories 677 | Fats 27.05g | Carbs 78.8g | Net Carbs 76.3g | Protein 34.88g

Bacon Jalapeño Poppers

Prep time: 5 minutes | Cook time: 45 minutes | Serves: 4

Ingredients:

5-Ingredients:

4 bacon slices, chopped

8 jalapeño peppers, halved lengthwise and deseeded

6 oz cream cheese, room temperature

¼ cup grated cheddar cheese

1 tbsp freshly chopped chives to garnish

Instructions

1. Select Sear/Sauté mode, adjust to Medium, and choose Start/Stop to preheat the pot for 5 minutes.
2. Add the bacon to the inner pot and cook until brown and crispy, 5 minutes. Transfer to a paper towel-lined plate to drain grease and clean the inner pot.
3. Return the pot to the base and close the Air Crisping Lid. Select Air Crisp, adjust to Medium High, and choose Start/Stop to preheat the lid for 5 minutes.
4. Lay the jalapeño peppers on a plate with open side up.
5. In a medium bowl, mix the cream cheese with the cheddar cheese and fill the mixture into the peppers. Top the cheese with the bacon.
6. Fix the Reversible Rack into the inner pot and arrange the peppers on top, cheese side up.
7. Close the Air Crisping Lid; select Air Crisp, adjust the temperature to 370 F and the timer to 5 minutes.
8. After cooking, transfer to a plate, garnish with the chives and serve warm as an appetizer.

Nutrition Facts per Serving

Calories 267 | Fats 22.56g | Carbs 10.25g | Net Carbs 8.85g | Protein 8.1g

Creamy Cilantro Polenta

Prep time: 10 minutes | Cook time: 6 minutes | Serves: 4

Ingredients:

5-Ingredients:

1 cup polenta

¼ cup freshly chopped cilantro

½ cup shredded cheddar cheese

¼ cup sour cream

2 tbsp heavy cream

Items from your pantry:

4 cups chicken broth

Salt to taste

4 tsp unsalted butter

Instructions

1. Select Sear/Sauté mode, adjust to Medium, and choose Start/Stop to preheat the pot for 5 minutes.
2. In the inner pot, mix the polenta and chicken broth and allow to start boiling.
3. Cover with the Pressure Lid and lock the vent to Seal. Select Pressure, adjust to High and set the timer to 7 minutes. Press Start to begin cooking.
4. After cooking, perform a natural pressure release for 5 minutes, then a quick pressure release to let out all the steam and open the lid.
5. Select Sear/Sauté mode, adjust to Medium, and choose Start/Stop.
6. Stir in the cilantro, butter, cheddar cheese, sour cream, and heavy cream until the cheese melts and the ingredients well combined.
7. Dish the food and serve as a side dish.

Nutrition Facts per Serving

Calories 629 | Fats 30.03g | Carbs 22.77g | Net Carbs 22.17g | Protein 63.27g

Sweet Butter Carrots

Prep time: 10 minutes | Cook time: 2 minutes | Serves: 4

Ingredients:

2-Ingredients:

3 large carrots, cut into chunks

1 tbsp freshly chopped parsley

Items from your pantry:

1 cup vegetable stock

2 tbsp honey

¼ cup butter, melted

Salt and freshly ground black pepper to taste

Instructions

1. In the inner pot, combine the carrots and vegetable stock.
2. Cover with the Pressure Lid and lock the vent to Seal. Select Pressure, adjust to High and set the timer to 2 minutes. Press Start to begin cooking.
3. After cooking, perform a quick pressure release to let out all the steam and open the lid.
4. Using a slotted spoon, remove the carrots into a medium bowl.
5. Top with the honey, butter, parsley, salt, and black pepper. Toss well.
6. Serve the carrots as a side dish.

Nutrition Facts per Serving

Calories 166 | Fats 12.13g | Carbs 13.89g | Net Carbs 12.29g | Protein 2g

Spicy Feta Potatoes

Prep time: 15 minutes | Cook time: 15 minutes | Serves: 4

Ingredients:

4-Ingredients:

1 ½ cups chopped Yukon Gold potatoes

4 oz crumbled feta cheese

½ cup roasted red bell peppers, diced

1 small yellow bell pepper, chopped and steamed

1 tbsp freshly chopped parsley

Items from your pantry:

2 tbsp olive oil

Salt to taste

½ jar of hot sauce

Instructions

1. Close the Air Crisping Lid and select Air Crisp; adjust the temperature to 375°F and the time to 5 minutes. Press Start to preheat.
2. Meanwhile, pour the potatoes in the Cook & Crisp basket and drizzle with the olive oil. Season with salt and toss.
3. Put the basket in the inner pot. Close the Crisping Lid; select Air Crisp, adjust the temperature to 375°F and the cook time to 15 minutes. Press Start to start frying.
4. After 8 minutes, open the lid, stir the potatoes and continue cooking. Remove the basket after cooking making sure that the potatoes are tender within. Otherwise, cook for 5 more minutes or until tender.
5. Open the lid and pour the potatoes into a large bowl.
6. Top with the feta cheese, bell peppers, and hot sauce. Mix everything well.
7. Dish, garnish with the parsley and serve warm.

Nutrition Facts per Serving

Calories 275 | Fats 19.01g | Carbs 14.52g | Net Carbs 12.72g | Protein 12.17g

Cheesy Vegetable Rice

Prep time: 10 minutes | Cook time: 25 minutes | Serves: 4

Ingredients:

5-Ingredients:

1 cup basmati rice, rinsed

¼ cup frozen mixed vegetables

¼ cup grated Parmesan cheese

1 cup grated cheddar cheese

Items from your pantry:

½ tsp garlic powder

½ tsp onion powder

1 ½ cups chicken broth

Salt and freshly ground black pepper to taste

Instructions:

1. In the inner pot, add the rice, mixed vegetables, garlic powder, onion powder, chicken broth, salt, and black pepper.
2. Cover with the Pressure Lid and lock the vent to Seal. Choose Pressure, set to High, and the timer to 5 minutes. Choose Start/Stop to begin cooking.
3. After cooking, allow the pot to sit uncovered for 10 minutes, then perform a quick pressure release and open the lid.
4. Select Sear/Sauté mode, adjust to Medium, and choose Start/Stop.
5. Add the cheeses to the pot and stir as they melt into the rice.
6. Once melted, dish the food and serve as a side dish.

Nutrition Facts per Serving

Calories 520 | Fats 26.71g | Carbs 33.39g | Net Carbs 26.59g | Protein 44.56g

Mexican-Style Rice and Beans

Prep time: 10 minutes | Cook time: 17 minutes | Serves: 4

Ingredients:

5-Ingredients:

1 cup red kidney beans

1 cup brown rice

½ bunch cilantro, leaves and stems separated

1 avocado, halved, pitted, and sliced

1 large lime, cut into wedges

Items from your pantry:

2 cups vegetable broth

1 cup water

Salt and freshly ground black pepper to taste

1 cup salsa (store-bought)

Instructions:

1. In the inner pot, mix the beans, vegetable broth, water, salt, and black pepper.
2. Cover with the Pressure Lid and lock the vent to Seal. Choose Pressure, set to High, and the timer to 12 minutes. Choose Start/Stop to begin cooking.
3. After 12 minutes, perform a quick pressure release until all the steam is out and stir in the rice.
4. Cover the Pressure Lid and lock the vent to Seal. Choose Pressure, set to High, and set the timer to 5 minutes. Press Start to continue cooking.
5. After cooking, perform a quick pressure release to let out all the steam and open the lid.
6. Stir in the salsa, cilantro, avocado, lime, salt, and black pepper,
7. Dish the food onto serving plates and serve warm as a side dish.

Nutrition Facts per Serving

Calories 304 | Fats 10.86g | Carbs 47.12g | Net Carbs 40.82g | Protein 7.15g

Tangy Steamed Veggies

Prep time: 15 minutes | Cook time: 5 minutes | Serves: 4

Ingredients:

5-Ingredients:

1 lb green beans, trimmed

1 ½ lb medium russet potatoes, halved

½ lb carrots, peeled and cut into large chunks

1 lb asparagus, trimmed and cut into thirds

1 lemon, juiced

Instructions:

1. Pour 1 cup of water into the inner pot. Fix in the Reversible Rack in the lower position and arrange the green beans, potatoes, carrots, and asparagus on top.
2. Cover with the Pressure Lid and close the vent to Seal. Select Pressure, adjust to High, and set the timer to 5 minutes. Press Start to begin cooking.
3. Once done cooking, perform a quick pressure release and open the lid.
4. Use tongs to remove the vegetables into a large bowl and top with the lemon juice.
5. Toss well in the lemon juice and plate the food.
6. Serve warm as a side dish.

Nutrition Facts per Serving:

Calories 204 | Fats 0.92g | Carbs 45.52g | Net Carbs 36.72g | Protein 7.88g

Desserts Recipe

Tapioca Pudding

Prep time: 15 minutes | Cook time: 32 minutes | Serves: 4

Ingredients:

2-Ingredients:

1 cup tapioca pearls

2 eggs

Items from your pantry:

3 cups whole milk

¼ tsp salt

½ cup granulated sugar

1 tsp vanilla extract

Instructions:

1. In the inner pot, add the tapioca, milk, and salt.
2. Cover with the Pressure Lid and close the vent to Seal. Select Pressure, adjust to High, and set the timer to 5 minutes. Press Start to begin cooking.
3. After cooking, perform a natural pressure release for 15 minutes, then a quick pressure release to let out the remaining steam, and open the lid.
4. Beat the eggs in a medium bowl and mix in 2 tablespoons of the tapioca liquid until adequately mixed. Pour the mixture into the tapioca along with the sugar and vanilla.
5. Select Sear/Sauté mode, adjust to Medium, and choose Start/Stop to continue cooking the pudding while still mixing. Cook for 5 to 10 minutes.
6. Spoon the pudding into serving bowls, allow complete cooling, and chill for 1 hour.
7. Serve afterward.

Nutrition Facts per Serving:

Calories 526 | Fats 17.19g | Carbs 70.81g | Net Carbs 70.51g | Protein 20.77g

New York Style Cheesecake

Prep time: 15 minutes| Cook time: 56 minutes + 4 hours chilling | Serves: 4

Ingredients:

5-Ingredients:

12 graham crackers

16 oz cream cheese, softened

½ cup sour cream

2 eggs

2 tbsp arrowroot starch

Items from your pantry:

1 ½ tbsp brown sugar

2 tbsp melted salted butter

1 cup granulated sugar

1 tsp vanilla extract

2 pinches salt

Instructions:

1. Pour the graham crackers into a plastic bag and gently crush by pounding with a rolling pin.
2. Pour the biscuit into a medium bowl and mix in the brown sugar and butter. Spoon the mixture into a 7-inch springform pan and use a spoon to press the mixture to fit into the bottom of the pan.
3. Pour 1 cup of water into the inner pot. Fix in the Reversible Rack in the lower position and place the cake pan on top.
4. Close the Air Crisping Lid; select Air Crisp; adjust the temperature to 350°F and the time to 6 minutes. Press Start and bake until set. Remove the cake pan and allow the crust to cool.
5. In a large bowl, using an electric hand mixer, whisk the cream cheese and granulated sugar until smooth. Mix in the sour cream, eggs, arrowroot starch, vanilla, and salt.
6. Pour the filling onto the crust and use a spatula to spread evenly. Cover the pan with foil and place the cake pan on the rack.
7. Cover with the Pressure Lid and lock the vent to Seal. Select Pressure; adjust to High and the time to 25 minutes. Press Start.
8. After cooking, perform a natural pressure release for 10 minutes, and then a quick pressure release to let out any remaining pressure.
9. Carefully open the lid and remove the cheesecake from the pot. Remove the foil.
10. Allow the cake to rest for 10 to 15 minutes and then chill in the refrigerator for 3 to 4 hours.
11. Slice and serve when ready to enjoy.

Nutrition Facts per Serving:

Calories 745   Fats 53.39g | Carbs 41.37g | Net Carbs 40.97g | Protein 25.01g

Yellow Cake Pineapple Upside Down

Prep time: 15 minutes | Cook time: 38 minutes | Serves: 4

Ingredients:

5-Ingredients:

1 (18.50 oz) box yellow cake mix

1 cup pineapple slices

Items from your pantry:

2 tbsp butter

¼ cup brown sugar

Instructions:

1. In a medium bowl, prepare the cake mix according to the instruction on box. Set aside.
2. Grease a 7-inch springform pan with butter, sprinkle the brown sugar at the bottom of the pan and arrange the pineapple slices on top. Pour the cake batter all over and cover the cake pan with foil.
3. Pour 1 ½ cups of water into the inner pot, fix in the Reversible Rack, and place the cake pan on top.
4. Cover with the Pressure Lid and lock the vent to Seal. Select Pressure; adjust to High and the time to 18 minutes. Press Start.
5. After cooking, perform a natural pressure release for 10 minutes, then a quick pressure release and carefully open the lid.
6. Carefully remove the cake pan, remove the foil, and allow cooling for 10 minutes.
7. Invert the cake onto a plate, slice, and serve.

Nutrition Facts per Serving:

Calories 670 | Fats 13.01g | Carbs 133.44g | Net Carbs 131.24g | Protein 6.5g

Raspberry Cheesecake

Prep time: 20 minutes| Cook time: 56 minutes + 4 hours of chilling | Serves: 4

Ingredients:

5-Ingredients:

12 graham crackers

16 oz cream cheese, softened

2 eggs

½ cup heavy cream

12 large fresh raspberries, mashed + more for garnishing

Items from your pantry:

2 tbsp brown sugar

2 tbsp melted butter

1 cup granulated sugar

2 tsp cinnamon powder

1 tsp vanilla extract

3 tbsp maple syrup

Instructions:

1. Pour the graham crackers into a plastic bag and gently crush by pounding a rolling pin on top.
2. Transfer the biscuit to a medium bowl and mix in the brown sugar and butter. Spoon the mixture into a 7-inch springform pan and using a spoon press the mixture to fit into the bottom of the pan.
3. Pour 1 cup of water into the inner pot. Fix in the Reversible Rack in the lower position and place the cake pan on top.
4. Close the Air Crisping Lid; select Air Crisp; adjust the temperature to 350°F and the time to 6 minutes. Press Start and bake until set. Remove the cake pan and allow the crust to cool.
5. In a large bowl, using an electric hand mixer, whisk the cream cheese and granulated sugar until smooth. Beat in the eggs, heavy cream, raspberries, cinnamon powder, vanilla extract, and maple syrup.
6. Pour the mixture onto the crust and use a spatula to spread evenly. Cover the pan with foil and place the cake pan on the rack.
7. Cover with the Pressure Lid and lock the vent to Seal. Select Pressure; adjust to High and the time to 25 minutes. Press Start.
8. After cooking, perform a natural pressure release for 10 minutes, and then a quick pressure release to let out any remaining pressure.
9. Carefully open the lid and remove the cheesecake from the pot. Remove the foil.
10. Allow the cake to rest for 10 to 15 minutes and then chill in the refrigerator for 3 to 4 hours.
11. Slice and serve when ready to enjoy.

Nutrition Facts per Serving:

Calories 679 | Fats 48.43g | Carbs 51.29g | Net Carbs 49.99g | Protein 11.95g

Caramel Popcorns

Prep time: 10 minutes | Cook time: 9 minutes | Serves: 4

Ingredients:

1-Ingredient:

1 cup sweet corn kernels

Items from your pantry:

4 tbsp butter

3 tbsp brown sugar

¼ cup whole milk

Instructions:

1. Select Sear/Sauté mode, adjust to High, and choose Start/Stop to preheat the pot for 5 minutes.
2. Melt the butter in the inner pot and mix in the corn kernels.
3. Cover the pot with a regular glass pot lid that is large enough to cover the pot.
4. The corns will begin popping afterward. Cook until all the corns have popped, 5 minutes. Transfer to a large serving bowl after.
5. Wipe the inner pot clean and return to the base.
6. Still in Sear/Sauté mode, combine the brown sugar and milk in the inner pot. Cook with frequent stirring until the sugar dissolves and the sauce coats the back of the spoon, 3 to 4 minutes.
7. Drizzle the caramel sauce all over the popcorns and mix to coat well.
8. Cool for a few minutes and serve afterward.

Nutrition Facts per Serving:

Calories 189 | Fats 14.06g | Carbs 14.14g | Net Carbs 13.24g | Protein 3.13g

Chocolate Crème de Pot

Prep time: 15 minutes| Cook time: 19 minutes + 6 hours of chilling | Serves: 4

Ingredients:

5-Ingredients:

1 ½ cups heavy cream

5 large egg yolks

¼ cup chocolate, melted

Items from your pantry:

½ cup whole milk

A pinch of salt

Instructions:

Whipped cream for topping

1 tbsp chocolate sprinkles for garnishing

¼ cup caster sugar

1. Select Sear/Sauté mode, adjust to High, and choose Start/Stop to preheat the pot for 5 minutes.
2. Pour the heavy cream and milk into the inner pot and allow boiling.
3. Meanwhile, in a medium bowl, beat the egg yolks, salt, and sugar until well combined.
4. Gradually, whisk the egg mixture into the cream until well mixed. Also, stir in the melted chocolate and cook until thickened, 2 to 3 minutes.
5. Spoon the mixture into 4 medium ramekins and set side. Clean the inner pot and return to the base.
6. Pour 1 cup of water into the inner pot, fix in the Reversible Rack in the lower position in the inner pot and arrange 3 ramekins on the rack making sure that their edges touch each other to make a stand for the last ramekin. Place the fourth ramekin on top.
7. Cover with the Pressure Lid and lock the vent to Seal. Select Pressure; adjust to High and the time to 6 minutes. Press Start.
8. After cooking, perform a natural pressure release for 10 minutes, then a quick pressure release to let out any remaining pressure, and open the lid.
9. Use tongs to carefully remove the cups onto a flat surface and cool completely. Chill further in the refrigerator for at least 6 hours.
10. To serve, top the dessert with some whipping cream and decorate with the chocolate sprinkles.

Nutrition Facts per Serving:

Calories 394 | Fats 26.88g | Carbs 32.62g | Net Carbs 31.92g | Protein 6.28g

Apricots Dulche de Leche

Prep time: 10 minutes | Cook time: 55 minutes | Chilling time: 1 hour | Serves: 4

Ingredients:

2-Ingredients:

2 cups sweetened condensed milk

4 apricots, halved, cored, and sliced

Instructions:

1. Divide the condensed milk into 4 medium ramekins.
2. Pour 2 cups of water into the inner pot, fix in the Reversible Rack in the lower position, and place the ramekins on top.
3. Cover with the Pressure Lid and lock the vent to Seal. Select Pressure; adjust to High and the time to 25 minutes. Press Start to cook.
4. After cooking, perform a natural pressure release for 30 minutes, and then a quick pressure release to let out any remaining pressure, and open the lid.
5. Remove the ramekins onto a flat surface and allow complete cooling.
6. After, use a fork to whisk the mixture until creamy and then, chill in the refrigerator for 1 hour.
7. To serve, top with the apricots and enjoy.

Nutrition Facts per Serving:

Calories 108 | Fats 4.02g | Carbs 14.42g | Net Carbs 13.82g | Protein 4.06g

Blackberry Cobbler

Prep time: 15 minutes | Cook time: 15 minutes | Serves: 4

Ingredients:

1-Ingredient:

4 cups fresh blackberries

Items from your pantry:

2 tbsp + ¾ cup plain flour, divided	1 ½ tsp salt, divided
½ cup + ¼ cup brown sugar, divided	¼ cup water
¼ tsp nutmeg powder	½ tsp baking powder
½ tsp cinnamon powder	½ tsp baking soda
1 tsp vanilla extract	3 tbsp butter, melted

Instructions:

1. In a large ramekin, mix the blackberries, 2 tbsp of flour, ½ cup of brown sugar, nutmeg, cinnamon, vanilla, ½ teaspoon of salt, and water. Set aside.
2. Pour 1 cup of water in the inner pot, fix in the Reversible Rack, and place the ramekin on top.
3. Cover with the Pressure Lid and lock the vent to Seal. Select Pressure; adjust to High and the time to 3 minutes. Press Start.
4. After cooking, perform a quick pressure release to let out the remaining steam, and open the lid.
5. In another bowl, mix the remaining flour, brown sugar, salt, baking powder, baking soda, and butter. Spoon the mixture over the blackberry mixture and spread evenly on top to cover the filling.
6. Close the Air Crisping Lid and select Bake/Roast; adjust the temperature to 325°F and the time to 12 minutes. Press Start.
7. After 8 minutes; check if the dough is cooking right and continue cooking.
8. When the timer is done, the topping should be lightly browned and cooked through. Allow cooling before slicing. Serve warm.

Nutrition Facts per Serving:

Calories 649 | Fats 9.67g | Carbs 134.57g | Net Carbs 123.97g | Protein 9.96g

Mango Rice Pudding

Prep time: 10 minutes | Cook time: 15 minutes | Serves: 4

Ingredients:

2-Ingredients:

1 cup jasmine rice

1 small mango, peeled and chopped into small bits

Items from your pantry:

1 tsp vanilla extract

½ tsp nutmeg powder

2 cups whole milk

1 tbsp unsalted butter

1/3 cup granulated sugar

A pinch of salt

Instructions:

1. Select Sear/Sauté mode, adjust to Medium High, and choose Start/Stop to preheat the pot for 5 minutes.
2. In the inner pot, mix the rice, mango, vanilla, nutmeg, milk, butter, sugar, and salt.
3. Cover with the Pressure Lid and lock the vent to Seal. Select Pressure; adjust to High and the time to 5 minutes. Press Start to cook.
4. After cooking, perform a natural pressure release for 10 minutes, then a quick pressure release to let out the steam, and open the lid.
5. Stir and adjust the taste with sugar.
6. Spoon into serving bowls and serve warm or chilled.

Nutrition Facts per Serving:

Calories 282 | Fats 12.09g | Carbs 45.09g | Net Carbs 38.19g | Protein 8.03g

Baked Stuffed Apples

Prep time: 15 minutes | Cook time: 5 minutes | Serves: 4

Ingredients:

5-Ingredients:

1/3 cup raisins

1/3 cup toasted pecans, chopped

1/3 cup dates, chopped

6 red apples, whole and cored

4 tbsp chocolate sauce for topping

Items from your pantry:

2 tbsp brown sugar

4 tbsp butter

1 tbsp. cinnamon powder

Instructions:

1. Close the Air Crisping Lid and select Bake/Roast; adjust the temperature to 325°F and the time to 5 minutes. Press Start to preheat the lid.

2. In a medium bowl, mix the raisins, pecans, dates, brown sugar, butter, and cinnamon. Stuff the apples with the mixture.

3. After the lid has preheated, pour 1 cup of water into the inner pot, fix in the Reversible Rack in the lower position, and put the apples on top.

4. Close the Air Crisping Lid and select Bake/Roast; adjust the temperature to 325°F and the time to 5 minutes. Press Start.

5. Open the lid after cooking and use tongs to lift the apples onto serving plates carefully.

6. Swirl the chocolate sauce on the apples and serve immediately.

Nutrition Facts per Serving:

Calories 355 | Fats 17.84g | Carbs 53.18g | Net Carbs 44.58g | Protein 2.16g

Fish and Seafood Recipe

Rustic Seafood Pot

Prep time: 15 minutes | Cook time: 7 minutes | Serves: 4

Ingredients:

5-Ingredients:

2 celery stalks, chopped

½ lb. clams, scrubbed

½ lb. prepared squid rings

Items from your pantry:

2 tbsp olive oil

1 large white onion, chopped

2 garlic cloves, minced

4 white fish fillets, cut into 1-inch cubes

6 tomatoes, chopped

½ cup white wine

1 cup fish stock

Salt and freshly ground black pepper to taste

Instructions

1. Select Sear/Sauté mode, adjust to Medium High, and choose Start/Stop to preheat the pot for 5 minutes.
2. Heat the olive oil in the inner pot and sauté the celery and onion until softened, 3 minutes. Stir in the garlic and cook until fragrant, 30 seconds.
3. Meanwhile, quickly sort the clams out and discard any with broken shells or that won't open when tapped.
4. Pour the good clams into the inner pot as well as the squid, fish, white wine, tomatoes, fish stock, salt, and black pepper.
5. Cover with the Pressure Lid and lock the vent to Seal. Select Pressure, set to High, and set the time to 3 minutes. Choose Start/Stop to begin cooking.
6. After cooking, do a quick pressure release, and carefully open the lid.
7. Stir the stew and adjust the taste with salt and black pepper,
8. Dish into serving plates and serve warm with bread.

Nutrition Facts per Serving

Calories 830 | Fats 66.26g | Carbs 19.7g | Net Carbs 16.5g | Protein 38.16g

Spicy Fried Salmon with Avocado Salsa

Prep time: 18 minutes | Cook time: 10 minutes | Serves: 4

Ingredients:

5-Ingredients:

4 salmon fillets

1 large avocado, halved, pitted, and chopped

1 small red onion, chopped

1 large tomato, deseeded and chopped

2 tbsp freshly chopped cilantro

Items from your pantry:

1 cup panko breadcrumbs

½ tsp cumin powder

½ tsp garlic powder

1 tsp chili powder

1 tsp smoked paprika

1 tsp salt

¼ tsp freshly ground black pepper

1 tbsp apple cider vinegar

Instructions:

1. Fix the Reversible Rack into the inner pot in the upper position.
2. Close the Air Crisping Lid; select Air Crisp, set the temperature to 390°F, and the time to 5 minutes. Choose Start/Stop to preheat the lid.
3. Meanwhile, in a large zipper bag, add the breadcrumbs, cumin powder, garlic powder, chili powder, paprika, salt, and black pepper. Close the bag and shake well to mix the seasoning.
4. Place the salmon in the bag (two pieces at a time) and shake to coat well with the seasoned crumbs.
5. After the lid has preheated, open and lay the fish on the rack; grease lightly with cooking spray.
6. Close the Air Crisping Lid; select Air Crisp, set the temperature to 390°F, and the time to 10 minutes. Choose Start/Stop to begin cooking the fish and flip halfway of the cooking time.
7. While the fish cooks, in a medium bowl, mix the avocado, onion, tomato, cilantro, and apple cider vinegar.
8. Serve the fish with the salsa when ready.

Nutrition Facts per Serving:

Calories 506 | Fats 21.7g | Carbs 8.8g | Net Carbs 4.1g | Protein 67.09g

Shrimp Bisque

Prep time: 15 minutes | Cook time: 15 minutes | Serves: 4

Ingredients:

5-Ingredients:

2 medium carrots, peeled and chopped

2 celery stalks, chopped

½ cup diced tomatoes

1 ½ cups medium shrimp, peeled, deveined, and chopped

1 cup heavy cream

Items from your pantry:

1 tbsp butter

1 small red onion, chopped

2 garlic cloves, minced

2 ½ cup chicken broth

1 tsp Old Bay seasoning

Salt and freshly ground black pepper to taste

5 tsp paprika

1 tsp dried dill

Instructions:

1. Select Sear/Sauté on the pot and set to Medium High. Choose Start/Stop to preheat the pot for 5 minutes.
2. Melt the butter in the inner pot and sauté the carrots, celery, and onion until softened, 3 minutes. Mix in the garlic and cook until fragrant, 30 seconds.
3. Stir in the tomatoes, chicken broth, Old Bay seasoning, salt, black pepper, paprika, dill, and shrimp.
4. Cover with the Pressure Lid and lock the vent to Seal. Select Pressure, adjust to High, and set the time to 10 minutes. Select Start/Stop to begin cooking.
5. When done cooking, perform a quick pressure release and carefully open the Pressure Lid.
6. Use a slotted spoon to fetch out the shrimp onto a plate and set aside.
7. Using an immersion blender, puree the soup until smooth and mix in the heavy cream.
8. Spoon the soup into serving bowls and top with the shrimp.
9. Serve warm with bread.

Nutrition Facts per Serving:

Calories 177 | Fats 14.84g | Carbs 9.53g | Net Carbs 6.83g | Protein 3.24g

Fried Scallops in Cilantro Sauce

Prep time: 15 minutes | Cook time: 5 minutes | Serves: 4

Ingredients:

4-Ingredients:

2 cups fresh cilantro leaves

1 lemon, zested and juiced

Items from your pantry:

2 tbsp unsalted butter

4 garlic cloves, minced

1 tbsp Dijon mustard

3 tbsp heavy cream

1 lb. scallops, tendons removed

Salt and freshly ground black pepper to taste

½ cup chicken broth

2 tbsp olive oil

Instructions:

1. Select Sear/Sauté on the pot and set to Medium High. Choose Start/Stop to preheat the pot for 5 minutes.
2. Melt the butter in the inner pot and stir in the cilantro and garlic. Cook until fragrant, 30 seconds. Mix in the lemon zest, lemon juice, Dijon mustard, salt, black pepper, and chicken broth.
3. Cover with the Pressure Lid and lock the vent to Seal. Select Pressure, set to High and set the time to 2 minutes. Choose Start/Stop to begin cooking.
4. After cooking, perform a quick pressure release and open the lid. Then, use an immersion blender to puree the ingredients until smooth.
5. Fix the Reversible Rack over the sauce in the upper position. Season the scallops with salt, black pepper, and arrange on the rack in a single layer; brush with the butter.
6. Close the Air Crisping Lid; select Air Crisp, set the temperature to 390°F, and the time to 2 minutes. Choose Start/Stop to begin cooking the scallops.
7. After 1 minute, open the lid and turn the scallops. Brush with a little more butter and continue cooking with the lid closed.
8. After the timer ends, open the lid and plate the scallops. Remove the rack and top the food with the sauce.
9. Serve warm.

Nutrition Facts per Serving:

Calories 225 | Fats 15.61g | Carbs 6.4g | Net Carbs 5.51g | Protein 14.89g

Breaded Trout with Parsley Pesto

Prep time: 15 minutes | Cook time: 10 minutes | Serves: 4

Ingredients:

5-Ingredients:

4 trout fillets

1 lemon, juiced

2 cups fresh parsley leaves

2 tbsp toasted pine nuts

3 tbsp grated Parmesan cheese

Items from your pantry:

1 cup panko breadcrumbs

Salt and freshly ground black pepper to taste

¼ tsp dried oregano

1 tsp lemon pepper

2 garlic cloves, minced

Salt to taste

¼ cup olive oil

Instructions:

1. Fix the Reversible Rack into the inner pot in the upper position.
2. Close the Air Crisping Lid; select Air Crisp, set the temperature to 390°F, and the time to 5 minutes. Choose Start/Stop to preheat the lid.
3. Meanwhile, in a large zipper bag, add the breadcrumbs, salt, black pepper, and oregano. Close the bag and shake well to mix the seasoning.
4. Place the fish in the bag (two pieces at a time) and shake to coat well with the seasoned crumbs. Remove the fish onto a plate and season both sides with the lemon pepper.
5. After the lid has preheated, open and lay the fish on the rack in a single layer; grease lightly with cooking spray.
6. Close the Air Crisping Lid; select Air Crisp, set the temperature to 390°F, and the time to 10 minutes. Choose Start/Stop to begin cooking the fish and flip halfway of the cooking time.
7. While the fish cooks, in a food processor, combine the parsley, garlic, pine nuts, Parmesan cheese, salt, and olive oil. Blend until smooth.
8. Plate the fish when ready and top with some pesto to taste.
9. Serve immediately.

Nutrition Facts per Serving:

Calories 402 | Fats 30.19g | Carbs 12.52g | Net Carbs 6.12g | Protein 21.89g

Paprika Tuna Cakes

Prep time: 15 minutes | Cook time: 27 minutes | Serves: 4

Ingredients:

5-Ingredients:

2 medium potatoes, peeled and chopped

4 (7 oz) cans tuna in oil, drained

1 scallion, chopped

1 egg, beaten

1 tbsp freshly chopped dill

Items from your pantry:

1 tsp cayenne pepper

4 tbsp plain flour

Salt and freshly ground black pepper to taste

Instructions:

1. Pour 1 cup of water with the potatoes into the inner pot.
2. Cover with the Pressure Lid and lock the vent to Seal. Select Pressure, adjust to High, and set the time to 12 minutes. Select Start/Stop to begin cooking.
3. After cooking, perform a quick pressure release and carefully open the lid.
4. Drain the potatoes through a colander, transfer to a large bowl, and clean the inner pot.
5. Place the Cook & Crisp Basket in the inner pot and close the Air Crisping Lid. Select Air Crisp, set the temperature to 375°F, and the time to 5 minutes. Select Start/Stop to preheat the pot.
6. Meanwhile, add to the potatoes the tuna, scallion, egg, dill, cayenne pepper, flour, salt, and black pepper. Use a potato masher to blend the ingredients and use your hands to form 4 large patties from the mixture.
7. Arrange the patties in the basket in a single layer and grease lightly with cooking spray.
8. Close the Air Crisping Lid. Select Air Crisp, set the temperature to 390°F, and the time to 10 minutes. Press Start/Stop to begin baking.
9. Halfway through the cook time, turn the fish cakes and continue cooking until the time reads to the end.
10. Transfer to serving plates when ready and serve warm.

Nutrition Facts per Serving:

Calories 669 | Fats 20.34g | Carbs 40.06g | Net Carbs 35.26g | Protein 77.74g

Red Wine Poached Salmon

Prep time: 15 minutes | Cook time: 11 minutes | Serves: 4

Ingredients:

4-Ingredients:

2 celery stalks, chopped

5 thyme sprigs

4 salmon fillets

2 tbsp freshly chopped parsley to garnish

Items from your pantry:

2 tbsp red wine vinegar

2 cups dry red wine

1 cup water

1 tbsp sugar

Salt and freshly ground black pepper to taste

Instructions:

1. In the inner pot, mix the celery, thyme, vinegar, red wine, water, sugar, salt, and black pepper. Place the fish in the liquid.
2. Cover with the Pressure Lid and lock the vent to Seal. Select Steam, adjust to High, and set the time to 3 minutes. Select Start/Stop to begin cooking.
3. After cooking, perform a quick pressure release and carefully open the lid.
4. Use tongs, to carefully remove the fish onto serving plates and set aside.
5. Select Sear/Sauté on the pot and set to Medium High. Choose Start/Stop to continue cooking the sauce until thickened, 5 to 8 minutes.
6. Spoon the sauce over the salmon, garnish with the parsley and serve warm.

Nutrition Facts per Serving:

Calories 441 | Fats 14.07g | Carbs 3.44g | Net Carbs 2.84g | Protein 65.52g

Garlic Lemon Shrimp with Asparagus

Prep time: 15 minutes | Cook time: 4 minutes | Serves: 4

Ingredients:

4-Ingredients:

1 cup chopped asparagus

½ lemon, juiced

1 lb. jumbo shrimp, peeled and deveined

2 tbsp freshly chopped parsley, to garnish

Items from your pantry:

1/3 cup butter, divided

4 garlic cloves, minced

Salt and freshly ground black pepper to taste

¼ tsp seafood seasoning

½ cup chicken broth

Instructions:

1. Select Sear/Sauté on the pot and set to Medium High. Choose Start/Stop to preheat the pot for 5 minutes.
2. Melt 4 tbsp of the butter in the inner pot and sauté the asparagus for 5 minutes until slightly softened. Mix in the garlic, season with salt and black pepper and cook until fragrant, 30 seconds.
3. Stir in the lemon juice, seafood seasoning, chicken broth, and place in the shrimp. Spoon the sauce to coat the shrimp.
4. Cover with the Pressure Lid and lock the vent to Seal. Select Pressure, set to High and set the time to 3 minutes. Choose Start/Stop to begin cooking.
5. After cooking, perform a quick pressure release until all the steam is out and open the lid.
6. Stir in the parsley, remaining butter and dish the food.

Nutrition Facts per Serving:

Calories 309 | Fats 18.89g | Carbs 3.17g | Net Carbs 2.27g | Protein 30.81g

Tuna in Mango Sauce

Prep time: 15 minutes | Cook time: 5 minutes | Serves: 4

Ingredients:

5-Ingredients:

1 cup chopped ripe mangoes

1 cup fresh mango juice

2 tsp freshly chopped basil

4 tuna fillets

2 tsp freshly chopped parsley

Items from your pantry:

2 tbsp butter

1 tbsp apple cider vinegar

1 tsp fresh ginger paste

1 medium red onion, finely chopped

¼ tsp red chili flakes

Salt and freshly ground black pepper to taste

Instructions:

1. Select Sear/Sauté on the pot and set to Medium High. Choose Start/Stop to preheat the pot for 5 minutes.
2. Melt the butter in the inner pot and mix in the mangoes, mango juice, basil, vinegar, ginger, onion, and red chili flakes.
3. Cover with the Pressure Lid and lock the vent to Seal. Select Pressure, set to High and set the time to 2 minutes. Choose Start/Stop to begin cooking.
4. After cooking, perform a quick pressure release and open the lid.
5. Fix the Reversible Rack over the sauce in the upper position. Season the tuna with salt, black pepper, and arrange in the rack in a single layer; grease with cooking spray.
6. Close the Air Crisping Lid; select Air Crisp, set the temperature to 390°F, and the time to 3 minutes. Choose Start/Stop to begin cooking the fish.
7. After 2 minutes, open the lid and turn the fish. Coat with a little more oil and continue cooking with the lid closed.
8. After the timer ends, open the lid and plate the tuna. Remove the rack and top the fish with the mango sauce.
9. Garnish with the parsley and serve warm.

Nutrition Facts per Serving:

Calories 519 | Fats 20.14g | Carbs 15.75g | Net Carbs 13.75g | Protein 66.36g

Mussel Stew with Red Wine

Prep time: 10 minutes | Cook time: 10 minutes | Serves: 4

Ingredients:

5-Ingredients:

1 lemon, zested and 2 tbsp juice

2 tbsp freshly chopped parsley

2 Roma tomatoes, diced

4 lemon wedges

1 ½ lb. fresh mussels, debearded and washed

Items from your pantry:

2 tbsp. unsalted butter

½ cup red wine

1 medium red onion, chopped

½ cup fish stock

4 garlic cloves, minced

Salt and freshly ground black pepper to taste

Instructions:

1. Select Sear/Sauté on the pot and set to Medium High. Choose Start/Stop to preheat the pot for 5 minutes.

2. Melt the butter in the inner pot and sauté the onion until softened, 3 minutes. Mix in the garlic and cook until fragrant, 30 seconds.

3. Mix in the lemon zest, lemon juice, tomatoes, red wine, fish stock, salt, and black pepper. Cook for 2 minutes and mix in the mussels.

4. Cover with the Pressure Lid and lock the vent to Seal. Select Pressure, adjust to High, and set the time to 4 minutes. Select Start/Stop to start cooking.

5. After cooking, perform a quick pressure release and carefully open the lid.

6. Spoon the mussels into serving bowls, discard any closed mussels, and spoon the sauce all over.

7. Garnish with the parsley and serve with the lemon wedges.

Nutrition Facts per Serving:

Calories 195 | Fats 4.35g | Carbs 16.01g | Net Carbs 14.51g | Protein 22.18g

Poultry Recipe

Pomegranate Chicken Tagine

Prep time: 15 minutes | Cook time: 37 minutes | Serves: 4

Ingredients:

5-Ingredients:

4 chicken thighs, bone-in

2 large carrots, peeled and chopped

15 oz canned chopped tomatoes with juice

½ cup frozen peas

1 tbsp pomegranate to garnish

Items from your pantry:

2 tbsp olive oil

Salt and freshly ground black pepper to taste

1 large onion, chopped

3 garlic cloves, minced

1 tsp fresh ginger puree

1 tbsp. balsamic vinegar

2 tbsp ras el hanout

1 tsp smoked paprika

1 tsp cumin powder

½ tsp cinnamon powder

1 cup chicken broth

Instructions

1. Select Sear/Sauté on the pot and set to Medium High. Choose Start/Stop to preheat the pot for 5 minutes.
2. Melt the olive oil in the inner pot, season the chicken on both sides with salt, black pepper, and cook in the oil until brown on both sides, 6 minutes. Plate and set aside.
3. Add the carrots and onion to the oil and cook until softened, 5 minutes. Stir in the garlic and ginger and cook until fragrant, 30 seconds.
4. Mix in the remaining ingredients except for the peas and pomegranate. Add the chicken and cover with the sauce.
5. Cover with the Pressure Lid and lock the vent to Seal. Select Pressure; adjust to High and the time to 10 minutes. Press Start to begin cooking.
6. After cooking, perform a natural pressure release for 10 minutes, then a quick pressure release and carefully open the lid.
7. Stir the peas into the sauce and keep the Foodi in Warm mode for 4 to 5 minutes or until the peas warm through.
8. Dish the tagine into serving bowls and garnish with the pomegranate.
9. Serve warm.

Nutrition Facts per Serving

Calories 716 | Fats 45.11g | Carbs 29.33g | Net Carbs 21.73g | Protein 48.69g

Adobo Drumsticks

Prep time: 15 minutes | Cook time: 25 minutes | Serves: 4

Ingredients:

3-Ingredients:

1 lb. chicken drumsticks

½ tsp freshly chopped Mexican oregano

2 tbsp freshly chopped cilantro to garnish

Items from your pantry:

½ cup soy sauce

2 tbsp olive oil

1 tsp chili powder

2 tsp garlic powder

½ tsp cumin powder

A pinch clove powder

Salt and freshly ground black pepper to taste

¼ cup apple cider vinegar

Instructions

1. Pour 1 cup of water into the inner pot and fix the Reversible Rack in the lower position of the pot. Place the chicken drumsticks on the rack.
2. Cover with the Pressure Lid and lock the vent to Seal. Select Pressure; adjust to High and time to 10 minutes. Press Start to begin cooking the chicken.
3. Meanwhile, in a large bowl, mix the oregano, soy sauce, olive oil, chili powder, garlic powder, cumin powder, clove powder, salt, black pepper, and vinegar. Set aside.
4. After cooking, perform a quick pressure release, and carefully open the lid.
5. Remove the rack from the pot and empty the water in the pot. Return the pot to the base.
6. Close the Air Crisping Lid and Choose Air Crisp; adjust the temperature to 375°F and the time to 5 minutes. Press Start to preheat the lid.
7. While preheating, toss the chicken in the sauce until well coated. Place the chicken in the Cook & Crisp basket.
8. Put the basket in the inner pot and close the Air Crisping Lid. Choose Air Crisp and adjust the temperature to 375°F and the cook time to 15 minutes. Press Start.
9. Halfway through the cook, open the lid and use tongs to turn the drumsticks. Close the lid and continue crisping the chicken.
10. Place the chicken when ready, drizzle with some of the remaining sauce and garnish with the cilantro.
11. Serve warm.

Nutrition Facts per Serving

Calories 377 | Fats 23.87g | Carbs 16.23g | Net Carbs 14.43g | Protein 23.84g

Paprika Thighs with Summer Vegetables

Prep time: 15 minutes | Cook time: 25 minutes | Serves: 4

Ingredients:

5-Ingredients:

3 fresh rosemary sprigs

1 lb. chicken thighs

½ lb. asparagus, stems removed

2 large carrots, chopped

½ lb. baby russet potatoes, quartered

Items from your pantry:

3 tbsp olive oil

Salt and freshly ground black pepper to taste

2 tbsp smoked paprika

1 tsp garlic powder

1 tsp onion powder

1 tsp dried parsley

Instructions

1. Pour 1 cup of water and the rosemary sprig into the inner pot, fix the Reversible Rack in the lower position of the pot, season the chicken with salt, black pepper, and arrange the chicken thighs on the rack.
2. In a bowl, toss the asparagus, carrots, and potatoes with 1 tbsp of olive oil, salt, and black pepper. Arrange the vegetables around the chicken.
3. Cover with the Pressure Lid and lock the vent to Seal. Select Pressure; adjust to High and time to 10 minutes. Press Start to begin cooking the chicken and vegetables.
4. Meanwhile, in a small bowl, mix the remaining olive oil with salt, black pepper, paprika, garlic powder, onion powder, and parsley.
5. After cooking, perform a quick pressure release, and carefully open the lid.
6. Remove the rack from the pot with the chicken and vegetables and empty the water in the pot. Return the pot to the base.
7. Close the Air Crisping Lid and Choose Air Crisp; adjust the temperature to 375°F and the time to 5 minutes. Press Start to preheat the lid.
8. While preheating, brush the chicken with the paprika sauce on both sides. Make a bed of the vegetables in the Cook & Crisp basket and arrange the seasoned chicken on top.
9. Put the basket in the inner pot and close the Air Crisping Lid. Choose Air Crisp adjust the temperature to 375°F and the cook time to 15 minutes. Press Start.
10. Halfway through the cook, open the lid and use tongs to turn the chicken and vegetables. Close the lid and continue crisping the chicken.
11. Place the chicken and vegetables when ready and serve warm.

Nutrition Facts per Serving

Calories 425 | Fats 29.61g | Carbs 19.07g | Net Carbs 14.77g | Protein 22.21g

Mushroom and Chicken Cacciatore

Prep time: 15 minutes | Cook time: 31 minutes | Serves: 4

Ingredients:

5-Ingredients:

4 chicken breasts

1 cup sliced white button mushrooms

15 oz can diced tomatoes

Items from your pantry:

2 tbsp olive oil

Salt and freshly ground black pepper to taste

1 medium white onion, chopped

2 cups of kale, steamed

¼ cup grated Parmesan cheese

¼ tsp ginger paste

2 garlic cloves, minced

1/3 cup chicken broth

1 tbsp Italian seasoning

Instructions

1. Select Sear/Sauté on the pot and set to Medium High. Choose Start/Stop to preheat the pot for 5 minutes.
2. Heat the olive oil in the inner pot, season the chicken with salt and black pepper, and cook on both sides in the oil until brown, 5 minutes. Transfer to a plate and set aside.
3. Add the mushroom and onion to the oil and cook until softened, 5 minutes. Stir in the ginger, garlic, and cook until fragrant, 30 seconds.
4. Mix in the tomatoes, chicken broth, Italian seasoning, and chicken.
5. Cover with the Pressure Lid and lock the vent to Seal. Select Pressure; adjust to High and time to 10 minutes. Press Start to begin cooking.
6. After cooking, perform natural pressure release for 10 minutes, then a quick pressure release to let out the remaining steam, and open the lid.
7. Stir the food, adjust the taste with salt, black pepper, and stir in the kale.
8. Select Sear/Sauté on the pot and set to Medium. Choose Start/Stop to cook the kale until wilted.
9. Dish the cacciatore onto serving plates, garnish with the Parmesan cheese and serve warm.

Nutrition Facts per Serving

Calories 629 | Fats 35.82g | Carbs 9.72g | Net Carbs 6.62g | Protein 64.37g

Thai Chicken Curry Rice

Prep time: 15 minutes | Cook time: 31 minutes | Serves: 4

Ingredients:

5-Ingredients:

4 chicken thighs

2 cups basmati rice

2 medium carrots, julienned

2 tbsp freshly chopped cilantro to garnish

1 red bell pepper, deseeded and thinly sliced

Items from your pantry:

1 tbsp olive oil

1 garlic clove, minced

Salt and freshly ground black pepper to taste

1 tsp ginger paste

1 cup chicken broth

2 tbsp red curry paste

1 cup coconut milk

Instructions

1. Select Sear/Sauté on the pot and set to Medium High. Choose Start/Stop to preheat the pot for 5 minutes.
2. Heat the olive oil in the inner pot, season the chicken with salt and black pepper, and cook on both sides in the oil until brown, 5 minutes. Transfer to a plate and set aside.
3. Add the carrots, bell pepper and cook until softened, 5 minutes. Stir in the curry paste, garlic, and ginger paste; cook until fragrant, 30 seconds.
4. Add the rice, chicken broth, coconut milk, chicken, salt, and black pepper.
5. Cover with the Pressure Lid and lock the vent to Seal. Select Pressure; adjust to High and time to 10 minutes. Press Start to begin cooking.
6. After cooking, allow the pot to sit uncovered for 10 minutes, then release a quick pressure release, and open the lid.
7. Stir the cilantro into the rice and adjust the taste with salt and black pepper.
8. Dish the food onto serving plates and serve warm.

Nutrition Facts per Serving

Calories 735 | Fats 50.95g | Carbs 41.96g | Net Carbs 27.86g | Protein 44.09g

Chili-Mango Glazed Chicken

Prep time: 15 minutes | Cook time: 21 minutes | Serves: 4

Ingredients:

5-Ingredients:

1 lb. chicken breasts, halved

2 tbsp spicy mango chutney

1 medium mango, chopped

1 small red chili, minced

2 scallions, thinly sliced

Items from your pantry:

2 tbsp butter

Salt and freshly ground black pepper to taste

¼ cup chicken broth

Instructions

1. Select Sear/Sauté on the pot and set to Medium High. Choose Start/Stop to preheat the pot for 5 minutes.
2. Melt the butter in the inner pot, season the chicken with salt, black pepper, and sear in the grease until brown on both sides, 6 minutes.
3. Mix in the mango chutney, mango, red chili, and chicken broth.
4. Cover with the Pressure Lid and lock the vent to Seal. Select Pressure; adjust to High and time to 10 minutes. Press Start to begin cooking.
5. After cooking, perform a natural pressure release for 5 minutes, then a quick pressure release, and open the lid.
6. Stir and dish the chicken with sauce on top. Garnish with the scallions and serve warm.

Nutrition Facts per Serving

Calories 276 | Fats 16.44g | Carbs 7.28g | Net Carbs 6.58g | Protein 24.15g

Sesame Orange Chicken

Prep time: 10 minutes | Cook time: 32 minutes | Serves: 4

Ingredients:

4-Ingredients:

4 chicken breasts, cut into 1-inch cubes

1 orange, zested and juiced

Items from your pantry:

2 tbsp olive oil

Salt to taste

6 garlic cloves, minced

2 tbsp fresh ginger puree

1 tbsp dry white wine

¼ cup brown sugar

4 scallions, chopped for garnishing

1 tbsp sesame seeds for garnishing

¼ cup tamarind sauce or soy sauce

¼ cup honey

1 tbsp hot sauce

¼ cup chicken broth

2 tbsp cornstarch mixed with 2 tbsp orange juice

Instructions

1. Select Sear/Sauté on the pot and set to Medium High. Choose Start/Stop to preheat the pot for 5 minutes.
2. Heat the olive oil in the inner pot, season the chicken with salt, black pepper, and sear in the oil until brown on both sides, 6 minutes. Transfer to a plate and set aside.
3. Add the garlic and ginger to the oil; cook until fragrant, 30 seconds. Mix in the orange juice, white wine, brown sugar, tamarind sauce, honey, hot sauce, and chicken. Stir and allow simmering for 1 minute. Place the chicken in the sauce.
4. Put the Pressure Lid together and lock to Seal. Choose Pressure; adjust to High and the cook time to 12 minutes. Press Start.
5. After cooking, perform a natural pressure release for 10 minutes, then a quick pressure release to let out the pressure, and open the lid.
6. Select Sear/Sauté on the pot and set to Medium High. Choose Start to continue cooking.
7. Stir in the corn starch until well mixed and cook until the sauce is syrupy, 1 to 2 minutes.
8. Dish the chicken and top with the sauce. Garnish with the scallions, sesame seeds, and serve warm.

Nutrition Facts per Serving

Calories 790 | Fats 37.88g | Carbs 47.95g | Net Carbs 46.85g | Protein 63.29g

Balsamic-Rosemary Whole Chicken

Prep time: 10 minutes | Cook time: 32 minutes | Serves: 4

Ingredients:

3-Ingredients:

2 fresh rosemary sprigs

3 lb. whole chicken, cleaned and rinsed

1 lemon, zested and juiced

Items from your pantry:

6 garlic cloves, minced

Salt and freshly ground black pepper to taste

1 tbsp onion powder

½ tsp smoked paprika

2 tbsp olive oil

4 tbsp balsamic vinegar

Instructions

1. Pour 1 cup of water and the rosemary sprigs in the inner pot, fix in the Reversible Rack in the lower position of the pot, season the chicken with salt, black pepper, and onion powder on all sides of the body and cavity. Place the chicken on the rack.
2. Cover with the Pressure Lid and lock the vent to Seal. Select Pressure; adjust to High and time to 20 minutes. Press Start to begin cooking the chicken.
3. Meanwhile, in a small bowl, mix the paprika, olive oil, balsamic vinegar, lemon zest, and lemon juice.
4. After cooking, perform a quick pressure release, and carefully open the lid.
5. Brush the chicken with the balsamic mixture.
6. Close the Air Crisping Lid and select Air Crisp; adjust the temperature to 400°F and the time to 12 minutes. Press Start to start cooking.
7. Halfway through the cook, check the chicken to be sure the crisping is working well. You may brush the chicken with more of the balsamic glaze.
8. Once the timer is done, open the lid and carefully lift the chicken onto a serving plate.
9. Cut and serve warm.

Nutrition Facts per Serving

Calories 467   Fats 16.04g | Carbs 6.57g | Net Carbs 6.07g | Protein 69.79g

Chicken Parmigiana

Prep time: 10 minutes | Cook time: 29 minutes | Serves: 4

Ingredients:

5-Ingredients:

4 chicken thighs, boneless and skinless

6 cups tomato pasta sauce

10 oz rigatoni

1 cup grated Parmesan cheese

2 cups grated mozzarella cheese

Items from your pantry:

½ cup chicken broth

¼ tsp red chili flakes

Salt and freshly ground black pepper to taste

1 tsp dried thyme

1 tsp dried oregano

1 tsp garlic powder

Instructions

1. Cut the chicken into 1-inch cubes and place in the inner pot. Top with the tomato sauce, chicken broth, red chili flakes, salt, black pepper, thyme, oregano, and garlic powder.
2. Cover with the Pressure Lid and lock the vent to Seal. Select Pressure; adjust to High and the cook time to 7 minutes. Press Start to begin cooking.
3. After cooking, perform a natural pressure release for 10 minutes, then a quick pressure release and carefully open the lid.
4. Stir in the rigatoni and adjust the sauce's taste with salt and black pepper.
5. Cover with the Pressure Lid and lock the vent to Seal. Select Pressure; adjust to High and the cook time to 5 minutes. Press Start to begin cooking.
6. After cooking, perform a quick pressure release and carefully open the lid.
7. Stir the food and sprinkle the Parmesan and mozzarella cheeses well on top.
8. Close the Air Crisping Lid and select Broil; adjust the temperature to 375°F and the time to 8 minutes. Press Start to begin browning the cheese.
9. After 4 minutes, check the cheeses to be sure of melting and browning. If golden brown and melted, turn off the Foodi, otherwise, keep broiling until brown to your desire.
10. Dish the food and serve warm.

Nutrition Facts per Serving

Calories 1108 | Fats 43g | Carbs 94.07g | Net Carbs 67.87g | Protein 71.98g

Thai Sweet Chili Chicken

Prep time: 10 minutes | Cook time: 25 minutes | Serves: 4

Ingredients:

1-Ingredient:

4 chicken breasts

Items from your pantry:

1/3 cup ketchup

1/3 cup soy sauce

2 tbsp teriyaki sauce

2 tbsp sweet chili sauce

2 ½ tbsp brown sugar

1 tbsp freshly grated ginger

3 garlic cloves, minced

½ tsp onion powder

Salt and freshly ground black pepper to taste

¼ cup chicken broth

1 ½ tbsp cornstarch mixed with 4 tbsp of water

Instructions

1. In the inner pot, mix the ketchup, soy sauce, teriyaki sauce, chili sauce, brown sugar, ginger, garlic, onion powder, salt, black pepper, and chicken broth. Place the chicken in the sauce and coat with the sauce.

2. Cover with the Pressure Lid and lock the vent to Seal. Select Pressure; adjust to High and the cook time to 12 minutes. Press Start to begin cooking.

3. After cooking, perform a natural pressure release for 10 minutes, then a quick pressure release to let out the remaining steam, and open the lid.

4. Shred the chicken with two long forks and stir in the cornstarch mixture.

5. Select Sear/Sauté on the pot and set to Medium High. Choose Start/Stop to continue cooking the food until the sauce is syrupy, 2 to 3 minutes.

6. Dish the food and serve warm.

Nutrition Facts per Serving

Calories 607 | Fats 30.74g | Carbs 15.96g | Net Carbs 14.46g | Protein 63.29g

Beef, Lamb, and Pork Recipe

Short Ribs with Tomato-Fig Chutney

Prep time: 15 minutes | Cook time: 45 minutes | Serves: 4

Ingredients:

5-Ingredients:

4 bacon slices, chopped

1 lb cherry tomatoes, halved

¼ cup fig preserves

3 tbsp fresh thyme leaves

1 lb beef short ribs, cut into 4 ribs

Items from your pantry:

1 tbsp olive oil

1 medium white onion, chopped

3 garlic cloves, minced

2 cups beef broth

1 cup Marsala wine

Salt and freshly ground black pepper to taste

1 tsp onion powder

1 tsp garlic powder

2 tbsp melted butter

Instructions

1. Select Sear/Sauté on the pot and set to Medium High. Choose Start/Stop to preheat the pot for 5 minutes.
2. Add the bacon to the inner pot and cook until brown, 5 minutes. Transfer to a paper towel-lined plate to drain grease and set aside.
3. Heat the olive oil in the bacon fat and sauté the onion and garlic until softened and

fragrant, 3 minutes. Mix in the tomatoes, fig preserves, thyme, beef broth, and Marsala wine.

4. Fix the Reversible Rack in the inner pot in the lower position and over the sauce.
5. Season the ribs with salt, black pepper, onion powder, and garlic powder. Place the ribs on the rack in a single layer as much as possible.
6. Cover with the Pressure Lid and lock the vent to Seal. Select Pressure, set to High, and set the time to 20 minutes. Choose Start/Stop to begin cooking.
7. After cooking, brush the ribs with the butter and close the Air Crisping lid.
8. Select Broil and set the time to 12 minutes. Press Start/Stop to continue cooking the beef.
9. Open the lid halfway, turn the meat, close the lid, and continue cooking until brown to your desire.
10. Remove the ribs onto a plate and set aside for serving. Also, take out the rack and stir the chutney.
11. Select Sear/Sauté on the pot and set to Medium High. Choose Start/Stop to continue cooking the sauce until thickened, 4 to 5 minutes.
12. Serve the ribs with the chutney when ready.

Nutrition Facts per Serving

Calories 508 | Fats 30.67g | Carbs 30.25g | Net Carbs 26.05g | Protein 31.13g

Beef Meatballs in Honey-Orange Sauce

Prep time: 15 minutes | Cook time: 28 minutes | Serves: 4

Ingredients:

5-Ingredients:

1 ½ lb. ground beef

2 large eggs, lightly beaten

¼ cup evaporated milk

1/3 cup orange marmalade

2 tbsp freshly chopped scallions for garnishing

Items from your pantry:

½ cup panko breadcrumbs

1 tsp garlic powder

1 tsp cumin powder

2 shallots, finely chopped

Salt and freshly ground black pepper to taste

1 tsp + 1/3 cup honey

2 tbsp butter, melted

2 tbsp cornstarch

2 tbsp soy sauce

2 tbsp hot sauce

1/3 cup firmly packed brown sugar

1 tbsp Worcestershire sauce

½ cup chicken broth

Instructions

1. Fix the Cook & Crisp basket into the inner pot. Close the Air Crisping Lid. Select Air Crisp, set the temperature to 400°F, and the time to 5 minutes. Choose Start/Stop to preheat the lid.

2. Meanwhile, in a large bowl, combine the beef, breadcrumbs, eggs, milk, garlic powder, cumin powder, shallots, salt, black pepper, and 1 tsp of honey until well mixed. Mold 1 ½-inch meatballs from the mixture.

3. When the lid is done preheating, open and arrange the meatballs in the basket; grease with cooking spray.

4. Close the Air Crisping Lid. Select Air Crisp, set the temperature to 400°F, and the time to 15 minutes. Choose Start/Stop to start frying the meatballs.

5. Halfway through the cook, open the lid and turn the meatballs. Continue cooking until crispy, brown, and cooked within. Open the lid and remove the meatballs onto a serving plate. Set aside for serving. Remove the basket from the pot.

6. Select Sear/Sauté on the pot and set to Medium High. Choose Start/Stop to preheat the pot for 5 minutes.

7. Melt the butter in the inner pot and mix in the orange marmalade, corn starch, soy sauce, hot sauce, brown sugar, honey, Worcestershire sauce, and chicken broth until well mixed.

8. Allow simmering for 5 to 8 minutes or until the sauce becomes syrupy and slightly thickened.

9. Pour the meatballs into the sauce and coat well with the sauce.

10. Dish the food, garnish with the scallions, and serve warm.

Nutrition Facts per Serving

Calories 912 | Fats 37.7g | Carbs 100.1g | Net Carbs 99.1g | Protein 46.57g

Spicy Beef Pitas

Prep time: 15 minutes | Cook time: 39 minutes | Serves: 4

Ingredients:

5-Ingredients:

1 lb. beef stew meat, cut into strips

1 medium tomato, chopped

1 large cucumber, deseeded and chopped

Items from your pantry:

1 tbsp olive oil

Salt and freshly ground black pepper to taste

1 small white onion, chopped

3 garlic cloves, minced

4 whole pita breads, warmed

1 cup Greek yogurt

1 tsp dried oregano

2 tsp hot sauce

¼ cup beef broth

1 tsp dried dill

Instructions

1. Select Sear/Sauté and set to High. Choose Start/Stop to preheat the pot for 5 minutes.
2. Heat the olive oil in the inner pot, season the meat with salt, black pepper, and sear in the oil until brown, 5 minutes. Transfer the meat to a plate and set aside.
3. Add the onion to the oil and cook until softened, 3 minutes. Stir in the garlic, oregano and cook until fragrant, 30 seconds. Stir in the hot sauce and beef broth.
4. Cover with the Pressure Lid and lock the vent to Seal. Select Pressure and set to High. Set the time to 20 minutes. Choose Start/Stop to begin cooking.
5. When the timer is done, perform a natural pressure release for 10 minutes, then a quick pressure release, and carefully open the lid.
6. Stir in the tomato, cucumber, and spoon the mixture into the pita breads.
7. In a medium bowl, mix the dill and yogurt, and top on the pita filling.
8. Serve immediately.

Nutrition Facts per Serving

Calories 312 | Fats 11g | Carbs 24.28g | Net Carbs 20.78g | Protein 31.18g

Lamb Macaroni Casserole

Prep time: 15 minutes | Cook time: 26 minutes | Serves: 4

Ingredients:

5-Ingredients:

1 lb ground lamb

2 large celery stalks, chopped

10 oz dried macaroni

2 cups chopped tomatoes

3 cups grated cheddar cheese

Items from your pantry:

1 tbsp olive oil

Salt and freshly ground black pepper to taste

1 tsp garlic powder

1 medium brown onion, chopped

1 ½ cups chicken broth

Instructions

1. Select Sear/Sauté on the pot and set to High. Select Start/Stop to preheat the pot for 5 minutes.
2. Heat the olive oil in the inner pot and cook the lamb until brown, 5 minutes. Season with salt, black pepper, garlic powder, and top with the onion and celery. Cook further for 3 minutes or until the onion and celery soften, 3 minutes.
3. Mix in the macaroni, tomatoes, and chicken broth.
4. Cover with the Pressure Lid and lock the vent to Seal. Choose Pressure, set to High, and set the time to 15 minutes. Select Start/Stop to begin.
5. After cooking, perform a quick pressure release and carefully open the lid.
6. Select Sear/Sauté on the pot and set to High. Select Start/Stop to continue cooking the food.
7. Stir; adjust the taste with salt and black pepper and mix in the cheddar cheese to melt.
8. Once melted, dish the food and serve warm.

Nutrition Facts per Serving

Calories 1429 | Fats 62.64g | Carbs 105.36g | Net Carbs 101.56g | Protein 109.82g

Lamb, Mushroom, and Rice Mix

Prep time: 15 minutes | Cook time: 34 minutes | Serves: 4

Ingredients:

5-Ingredients:

1 lb. ground lamb	1 cup basmati rice
1 cup sliced cremini mushrooms	2 cups frozen mixed veggies
1 red bell pepper, deseeded and chopped	

Items from your pantry:

2 tbsp olive oil	1 tsp Italian seasoning
1 medium onion, chopped	¼ tsp chili powder
2 garlic cloves, minced	½ tsp cumin powder
2 ½ tbsp tomato paste	1 tsp onion powder
Salt and freshly ground black pepper to taste	1 bay leaf
	1 cup chicken broth

Instructions

1. Select Sear/Sauté on the pot and set to High. Select Start/Stop to preheat the pot for 5 minutes.
2. Heat the olive in the inner pot and cook until the lamb until brown, 5 minutes. Add the onion, mushrooms, bell pepper, and garlic until softened and fragrant, 4 minutes.
3. Mix in the tomato paste, salt, black pepper, Italian seasoning, chili powder, cumin powder, onion powder, and bay leaf. Cook for 2 minutes to release fragrance. Stir in the rice and chicken broth.
4. Cover with the Pressure Lid and lock the vent to Seal. Select Pressure, set to High, and set the time to 5 minutes. Select Start/Stop.
5. After cooking, allow the pot to sit uncovered for 10 minutes, then perform a quick pressure release, and open the lid.
6. Select Sear/Sauté on the pot and set to High. Select Start/Stop to continue cooking.
7. Mix in the vegetables and cook for 3 minutes or until the veggies warm through. Adjust the food's taste with salt and black pepper.
8. Dish and serve warm.

Nutrition Facts per Serving

Calories 508 | Fats 31.6g | Carbs 29.71g | Net Carbs 18.11g | Protein 37.9g

Lamb Rogan Josh

Prep time: 20 minutes | Cook time: 43 minutes | Serves: 4

Ingredients:

4-Ingredients:

2 pounds boneless lamb shoulder, cubed

1 (15 oz) can tomato sauce

8 tbsp plain yogurt

3 tbsp freshly chopped cilantro

Items from your pantry:

2 tbsp ghee

1 large onion, chopped

10 garlic cloves, minced

2 tsp minced ginger

Salt to taste and black pepper to taste

1 tsp garam masala

1 tsp turmeric

1 bay leaf

4 tsp chili powder

3 tsp coriander powder

½ tsp cinnamon powder

¼ tsp cumin powder

⅛ tsp ground cloves

½ tsp cardamom powder

¼ cup chicken broth

Instructions

1. Select Sear/Sauté on the pot and set to High. Select Start/Stop to preheat the pot for 5 minutes.
2. Melt the ghee in the inner pot, season the lamb with salt, black pepper, and cook in the oil until brown on both sides, 7 minutes. Stir in the onion and cook until softened, 3 minutes.
3. Mix in the garlic, ginger, salt, black pepper, garam masala, turmeric, bay leaf, chili powder, coriander powder, cinnamon powder, cumin powder, cloves powder, and cardamom powder. Cook until fragrant, 3 minutes. Stir in the tomatoes, yogurt, and chicken broth.
4. Cover with the Pressure Lid together and lock to Seal. Select Pressure, set to High, and set the time to 15 minutes. Select Start/Stop to continue cooking.
5. After cooking, perform a natural pressure release for 10 minutes, then a quick pressure release, and open the lid.
6. If the sauce is too runny, select Sear/Sauté on the pot and set to High. Select Start/Stop to continue cooking until the sauce thickens, 4 to 5 minutes.
7. Stir in the cilantro, dish and serve warm.

Nutrition Facts per Serving

Calories 482 | Fats 26.46g | Carbs 15g | Net Carbs 14.5g | Protein 48.49g

Lemon Pork Chops with Sriracha

Prep time: 15 minutes | Cook time: 45 minutes + 1 hour marinating | Serves: 4

Ingredients:

2-Ingredients:

4 boneless pork chops   1 lemon, juiced

Items from your pantry:

1 tbsp soy sauce   2 tbsp sesame oil

2 tbsp sriracha sauce   2 tbsp olive oil

Instructions

1. Put the pork chops in a large zipper bag. In a small bowl, mix the lemon juice, soy sauce, sriracha sauce, and sesame oil. Pour the mixture onto the pork, close the bag, and massage the spice mixture onto the pork until well coated. Allow marinating for 1 hour.
2. After 1 hour, pour 1 cup of water into the inner pot, fix the Reversible Rack in the inner pot in the lower position, remove the pork from the marinade, and place on the rack.
3. Cover with the Pressure Lid and lock the vent to Seal. Select Pressure, set to High, and set the time to 20 minutes. Choose Start/Stop to begin cooking.
4. After cooking, perform a natural pressure release for 10 minutes, then a quick pressure release, and open the lid.
5. Remove the meat onto a plate, reposition the rack to the upper position, and return the meat to the rack. Brush well with the olive oil.
6. Close the Air Crisping lid. Select Air Crisp; adjust the temperature to 400°F and the cook time to 15 minutes. Press Start to begin crisping the meat.
7. Open the lid halfway, turn the meat, brush with more olive oil, close the lid, and continue cooking until brown to your desire.
8. Remove the meat onto a serving plate when ready and serve warm.

Nutrition Facts per Serving

Calories 372   Fats 20.64g | Carbs 2.42g | Net Carbs 2.12g | Protein 41.92g

Pork Prosciutto and Corn Masala

Prep time: 15 minutes | Cook time: 53 minutes | Serves: 4

Ingredients:

5-Ingredients:

6 pieces prosciutto, chopped

4 boneless pork chops

2 small Yukon Gold potatoes, peeled and diced

1 ½ cups sweet corn kernels

3 tbsp heavy cream

Items from your pantry:

1 tbsp olive oil

Salt and freshly ground black pepper to taste

1 medium red onion, chopped

2 garlic cloves, minced

1 red chili pepper, deseeded and minced

½ cup Marsala wine

2 cups chicken broth

Instructions

1. Select Sear/Sauté and adjust to Medium-High. Press Start to preheat the pot for 5 minutes.
2. Cook the prosciutto in the inner pot until brown and crispy, 5 minutes. Transfer to a paper-towel-lined plate to drain grease and set aside.
3. Heat the olive oil in the bacon grease, season the pork with salt and black pepper, and brown in the oil on both sides until golden, 6 minutes. Transfer to a plate and set aside.
4. Sauté the onion, garlic, and red chili pepper in the oil until fragrant, 2 minutes. Stir in the wine, cook until reduced by one-third and mix in the chicken broth, potatoes, corn, pork, and prosciutto.
5. Cover with the Pressure Lid and lock the vent to Seal. Select Pressure; adjust to High and the cook time to 30 minutes. Press Start to begin cooking.
6. After cooking, perform a natural pressure release for 10 minutes, then a quick pressure release, and open the lid.
7. Remove the pork onto a plate and stir in the heavy cream. Adjust the taste with salt and black pepper,
8. Share the pork onto serving plates and spoon the sauce on top.
9. Serve warm.

Nutrition Facts per Serving

Calories 687 | Fats 30.98g | Carbs 47.07g | Net Carbs 40.97g | Protein 54.94g

Rosemary Lemon Pork Chops

Prep time: 15 minutes | Cook time: 50 minutes + 30 minutes | Serves: 4

Ingredients:

3-Ingredients:

1 lemon, juiced

4 rosemary sprigs

4 bone-in pork chops

Items from your pantry:

1 tbsp olive oil

2 tsp garlic powder

Salt and freshly ground black pepper to taste

½ tsp Dijon mustard

Instructions

1. In a medium bowl, mix the olive oil, salt, black pepper, garlic powder, Dijon mustard, and lemon juice. Brush the seasoning sauce on both sides of the pork, cover in plastic wrap and marinate in the refrigerator for 30 minutes.
2. After, pour 1 cup of water in the inner pot, fix in the Reversible Rack, unwrap the pork, and place on the rack. Arrange the rosemary sprigs in between and around the pork chops.
3. Cover with the Pressure Lid and lock the vent to Seal. Select Pressure, set to High, and set the time to 25 minutes. Choose Start/Stop to begin cooking.
4. After cooking, perform a natural pressure release for 10 minutes, then a quick pressure release, and open the lid.
5. Remove the meat onto a plate, reposition the rack to the upper position, and return the meat to the rack. Brush well with the remaining marinade.
6. Close the Air Crisping lid. Select Air Crisp; adjust the temperature to 400°F and the cook time to 15 minutes. Press Start to begin crisping the meat.
7. Open the lid halfway, turn the meat, close the lid, and continue cooking until brown to your desire.
8. Remove the meat onto a serving plate when ready and serve warm.

Nutrition Facts per Serving

Calories 366 | Fats 20.8g | Carbs 1.99g | Net Carbs 1.79g | Protein 40.53g

Tuscan Pork Chops

Prep time: 15 minutes | Cook time: 42 minutes | Serves: 4

Ingredients:

5-Ingredients:

4 pork chops, fat trimmed

1 ½ chopped tomatoes

1 tbsp freshly chopped basil

1 tbsp fresh sage leaves

½ cup pitted black olives

Items from your pantry:

1 tbsp olive oil

Salt and freshly ground black pepper to taste

1 large red onion, chopped

5 garlic cloves, minced

2 tsp dried oregano

½ cup chicken broth

Instructions

1. Select Sear/Sauté and adjust to Medium. Press Start to preheat the pot for 5 minutes.
2. Heat the olive oil in the pot, season the pork with salt, black pepper, and sear in the oil until golden brown, 6 to 8 minutes.
3. Stir in the onion and garlic; cook until fragrant and softened, 2 minutes. Mix in the oregano, tomatoes, basil, sage, and cook until fragrant, 2 minutes. Stir in the chicken broth.
4. Cover with the Pressure Lid and lock the vent to Seal. Select Pressure; adjust to High, and the cook time to 20 minutes. Press Start to continue cooking.
5. After cooking, perform a natural pressure release for 10 minutes, then a quick pressure release, and open the lid.
6. Stir in the olives, dish the food onto plates and serve warm.

Nutrition Facts per Serving

Calories 453 | Fats 24.65g | Carbs 7.99g | Net Carbs 5.99g | Protein 48.09g

Vegan, Vegetarian, and Vegetables Recipe

Vegan Vegetable Minestrone

Prep time: 15 minutes | Cook time: 15 minutes | Serves: 4

Ingredients:

5-Ingredients:

5 Yukon gold potatoes, peeled and diced

1 cup chopped tomatoes

4 celery stalks, chopped

1 bunch fresh parsley, chopped

4 medium carrots, peeled and chopped

Items from your pantry:

3 cups vegetable broth

1 tsp dried thyme

1 ½ cups water

1 tsp dried oregano

4 garlic cloves, minced

2 bay leaves

1 medium sweet onion

Salt and freshly ground black pepper to taste

Instructions

1. In the inner pot, mix the vegetable broth, water, potatoes, celery, carrots, tomatoes, garlic, onion, tomatoes, thyme oregano, bay leaves, salt, and black pepper.

2. Cover with the Pressure Lid and lock the vent to Seal. Select Pressure; adjust to High and the cook time to 10 minutes. Press Start.

3. After cooking, perform a natural pressure release for 5 minutes, then a quick pressure release, and open the lid.

4. Stir in the parsley, adjust the taste with salt and black pepper, and dish the soup.

5. Serve warm.

Nutrition Facts per Serving

Calories 456 | Fats 1.98g | Carbs 97.52g | Net Carbs 83.52g | Protein 15.32g

Vegetable Tart

Prep time: 15 minutes | Cook time: 7 minutes | Serves: 4

Ingredients:

5-Ingredients:

2 cups broccoli, grated

3 large zucchini, grated and drained

6 large carrots, grated

5 eggs, beaten

½ cup grated cheddar cheese

Items from your pantry:

1 onion, diced

Salt and freshly ground black pepper to taste

½ cup panko breadcrumbs

½ cup plain flour

½ tsp baking powder

Instructions

1. Pour 1 cup of water in the inner pot, fix in the Reversible Rack, and lightly grease a 7-inch springform pan with cooking spray. Set aside.

2. In a large bowl, mix all the ingredients until well combined, pour the mixture into the cake pan, and spread out evenly. Cover the pan with foil and place on the rack.

3. Cover with the Pressure Lid and lock the vent to Seal. Select Pressure; adjust to High and the cook time to 5 minutes. Press Start.

4. After cooking, perform a quick pressure release, and open the lid.

5. Take off the foil and close the Air Crisping lid. Select Broil; adjust the temperature to 375°F and the cook time to 2 minutes. Press Start.

6. Halfway through, check if the top of the tart is brown to your desire. If yes, stop cooking, otherwise cook to the end of the time.

7. Take out the pan and release the tart onto a plate.

8. Slice and serve warm.

Nutrition Facts per Serving

Calories 406 | Fats 18.92g | Carbs 34.92g | Net Carbs 30.32g | Protein 24.58g

Pappardelle with Tomatoes and Arugula

Prep time: 15 minutes | Cook time: 14 minutes | Serves: 4

Ingredients:

4-Ingredients:

2 cups dried pappardelle

1 cup cherry tomatoes, halved

A handful of baby arugula

1 cup grated vegan Parmesan cheese

Items from your pantry:

Salt and freshly ground black pepper to taste

2 tbsp olive oil

2 garlic cloves, minced

Instructions

1. In the inner pot, add the pasta, 4 cups of water, and salt.
2. Cover with the Pressure Lid and lock the vent to Seal. Select Pressure; adjust to High and the cook time to 3 minutes. Press Start.
3. After cooking, perform a quick pressure release, and open the lid.
4. Drain the pasta through a colander and set aside. Wipe the inner pot clean and return to the base.
5. Select Sear/Sauté and adjust to Medium. Press Start to preheat the pot for 5 minutes.
6. Heat the olive oil in the inner pot and cook the garlic until fragrant, 30 seconds.
7. Stir in the tomatoes and cook until slightly softened, 2 to 3 minutes. Mix in the pasta, and arugula. Season with salt and black pepper; cook until the arugula wilts, 1 to 2 minutes.
8. Dish the food onto serving plates and top with the Parmesan cheese.
9. Serve warm.

Nutrition Facts per Serving

Calories 293 | Fats 13.92g | Carbs 37.76g | Net Carbs 33.36g | Protein 8.07g

Tofu Taco Quinoa Bowls

Prep time: 10 minutes | Cook time: 20 minutes | Serves: 4

Ingredients:

5-Ingredients:

1 lb. firm tofu, pressed and crumbled

1 cup quinoa

1 (8 oz) can black beans, rinsed and drained

Items from your pantry:

1 tbsp olive oil

Salt and freshly ground black pepper to taste

2 garlic cloves, minced

1 onion, finely diced

1 (14 oz) can diced tomatoes

1 cup grated vegan cheddar cheese, grated

1 jalapeño pepper, minced

1 tbsp chili seasoning

1 tsp cumin powder

2 ½ cups vegetable broth

Instructions

1. Select Sear/Sauté and adjust to Medium. Press Start to preheat the pot for 5 minutes.
2. Heat the olive oil in the inner pot and cook the tofu until brown, 5 minutes.
3. Season with salt, black pepper, and stir in the garlic, bell peppers, onion, and jalapeño pepper. Cook until the vegetables soften, 5 minutes.
4. Season with the chili pepper, cumin powder, and mix in the quinoa, black beans, tomatoes, and vegetable broth.
5. Cover with the Pressure Lid and lock the vent to Seal. Select Pressure; adjust to High, and the cook time to 3 minutes. Press Start.
6. After cooking, perform a quick pressure, and open the lid.
7. Stir and adjust the taste with salt and black pepper, and dish the food onto serving plates.
8. Top with the cheddar cheese and serve warm.

Nutrition Facts per Serving

Calories 673 | Fats 29.35g | Carbs 63.47g | Net Carbs 53.47g | Protein 45.47g

Creamy Cheesy Fettucine

Prep time: 10 minutes | Cook time: 11 minutes | Serves: 4

Ingredients:

5-Ingredients:

16 oz dried fettuccine

1 cup heavy cream

1 cup grated Parmesan cheese + extra for serving

1 tbsp freshly chopped parsley

Items from your pantry:

2 tbsp butter

A pinch of nutmeg powder

Salt and freshly ground black pepper to taste

Instructions

1. In the inner pot, add the fettuccine, 4 cups of water, and salt.
2. Cover with the Pressure Lid and lock the vent to Seal. Select Pressure; adjust to High, and the cook time to 4 minutes. Press Start.
3. After cooking, perform a quick pressure release and open the lid.
4. Drain the pasta through a colander and set aside. Wipe the inner pot clean and return the pot to the base.
5. Select Sear/Sauté and adjust to Medium. Press Start to preheat the pot for 5 minutes.
6. Melt the butter in the inner pot and mix in the heavy cream, nutmeg, and Parmesan cheese until the cheese melts, 2 minutes. Season with salt and black pepper.
7. Add the fettuccine and mix with the sauce until well coated.
8. Dish the food and garnish with more Parmesan cheese and parsley
9. Serve warm.

Nutrition Facts per Serving

Calories 504   Fats 18.23g | Carbs 83.62g | Net Carbs 73.72g | Protein 9.76g

Moroccan Chickpea Curry

Prep time: 15 minutes | Cook time: 20 minutes | Serves: 4

Ingredients:

5-Ingredients:

2 ½ cups canned chickpeas, drained

½ cup chopped tomatoes

1 cup mixed chopped bell peppers

2 tbsp freshly chopped parsley

2 medium carrots, chopped

Items from your pantry:

1 large yellow onion, finely chopped

2 long, red chilies, minced

4 garlic cloves, minced

½ tsp turmeric powder

¾ cup vegetable broth

Salt and freshly ground black pepper to taste

2 tbsp ras el hanout

2 tsp dried thyme

Instructions

1. Select Sear/Sauté and adjust to Medium-High. Press Start to preheat the pot for 5 minutes.

2. In the inner pot, combine the chickpeas, bell peppers, carrots, tomatoes, onion, garlic, vegetable broth, ras el hanout, red chilies, turmeric, salt, black pepper, and thyme.

3. Cover with the Pressure Lid and lock the vent to Seal. Select Pressure; adjust to High, and the cook time to 10 minutes. Press Start.

4. After cooking, perform a natural pressure release for 10 minutes, then a quick pressure release and open the lid.

5. Stir in the curry and adjust the taste with salt and black pepper. Mix in the parsley and dish the food.

6. Serve warm.

Nutrition Facts per Serving

Calories 541 | Fats 10.76g | Carbs 87.99g | Net Carbs 70.79g | Protein 26.99g

Yellow Lentil Dhal with Spinach

Prep time: 10 minutes | Cook time: 28 minutes | Serves: 4

Ingredients:

4-Ingredients:

1 ½ cups dried yellow lentils, washed, drained

2 cups chopped tomatoes

2 cups chopped spinach

2 tbsp freshly chopped coriander

Items from your pantry:

1 tbsp ghee

1 tbsp cumin seeds

½ tsp cayenne powder

1 tsp mustard seeds

1 tbsp turmeric powder

1 onion, thinly sliced

3 garlic cloves, minced

1 tbsp freshly grated ginger

1 cup vegetable broth

1 tsp sugar

Instructions

1. Select Sear/Sauté and adjust to Medium-High. Press Start to preheat the pot for 5 minutes.
2. Melt the ghee in the inner pot and stir-fry the cumin seeds, cayenne powder, mustard seeds, and turmeric until fragrant, 1 minute.
3. Mix in the onion, garlic, and ginger; cook until the onion softens, 3 minutes.
4. Stir in the lentils, tomatoes, vegetable broth, and sugar.
5. Cover with the Pressure Lid and lock the vent to Seal. Select Pressure; adjust to High, and the cook time to 10 minutes. Press Start to begin cooking.
6. After cooking, perform a natural pressure release for 10 minutes, then a quick pressure release and open the lid.
7. Stir in the spinach and set the pot in Sear/Sauté mode on Medium temperature. Cook the stew further until the spinach wilts, 4 minutes.
8. Spoon the dhal into serving bowls and garnish with the coriander.
9. Serve warm.

Nutrition Facts per Serving

Calories 117 | Fats 2.21g | Carbs 23.19g | Net Carbs 18.99g | Protein 4.91g

Roasted Broccoli-Mushroom Plate with Almonds

Prep time: 10 minutes | Cook time: 5 minutes | Serves: 4

Ingredients:

4-Ingredients:

1 large head broccoli, cut into bite-size pieces

1 cup white button mushrooms

2 tbsp chopped almonds

1 tbsp freshly chopped parsley to garnish

Items from your pantry:

2 tbsp butter, melted

2 garlic cloves, minced

Salt and freshly ground black pepper to taste

Instructions

1. Place the Cook & Crisp basket in the inner pot and Close the Air Crisping Lid. Select Bake/Roast; adjust the temperature to 375°F and the time to 5 minutes to preheat the inner pot. Press Start to preheat the pot.
2. Meanwhile, in a medium bowl, toss the broccoli and mushrooms with the butter, garlic, salt, and black pepper.
3. When the pot has preheated, open the lid and pour the vegetables into the basket.
4. Close the Air Crisping Lid and select Bake/Roast; adjust the temperature to 375°F and the time to 5 minutes. Press Start to begin cooking.
5. Halfway through, stir the vegetables, close the lid, and continue roasting.
6. When ready, transfer the vegetables to a serving bowl and mix in the almonds. Garnish with the parsley and serve warm.

Nutrition Facts per Serving

Calories 114 | Fats 6.72g | Carbs 11.56g | Net Carbs 7.26g | Protein 5.34g

Tangy Green Beans with Peanuts

Prep time: 10 minutes | Cook time: 6 minutes | Serves: 4

Ingredients:

3-Ingredients:

1 lb. green beans, trimmed

1 lemon, juiced

2 tbsp toasted peanuts

Items from your pantry:

2 tbsp olive oil

Salt and freshly ground black pepper to taste

Instructions

1. Pour 1 cup of water in the inner pot, fix in the Cook & Crisp basket and pour the green beans into the basket.
2. Cover with the Pressure Lid and lock the vent to Seal. Select Pressure; adjust to High and the cook time to 3 minutes. Press Start.
3. After cooking, perform a quick pressure release, and open the lid.
4. In a small bowl, mix the lemon juice, olive oil, salt, and black pepper. Drizzle the mixture over the green beans and toss well to coat.
5. Close the Air Crisping Lid and select Broil; adjust the temperature to 375°F and the time to 3 minutes. Press Start to brown the green beans while stirring halfway.
6. After cooking, open the lid and remove the green beans onto serving plates.
7. Top with the peanuts and serve warm.

Nutrition Facts per Serving

Calories 134 | Fats 10.36g | Carbs 8.94g | Net Carbs 6.24g | Protein 3.64g

Steamed Cabbage Wedges with Chili Lemon Dressing

Prep time: 5 minutes | Cook time: 3 minutes | Serves: 4

Ingredients:

2-Ingredients:

1 large cabbage, cut into wedges

1 lemon, juiced

Items from your pantry:

¼ tsp red chili flakes

1 tsp Dijon mustard

2 tbsp butter, melted

Salt and freshly ground black pepper to taste

Instructions

1. Pour the 1 cup of water in the inner pot, fix in the Reversible Rack in the lower position, and lay place the cabbage wedges on the rack.
2. Cover with the Pressure Lid and lock the vent to Seal. Select Pressure; adjust to High and the time to 3 minutes. Press Start.
3. After cooking, perform a quick pressure release, and open the lid.
4. Remove the cabbage onto a plate and set aside.
5. In a medium bowl, whisk the lemon juice, chili flakes, Dijon mustard, butter, salt, and black pepper until well combined.
6. Drizzle the mixture all over the cabbage and serve immediately.

Nutrition Facts per Serving

Calories 143 | Fats 6.31g | Carbs 21.89g | Net Carbs 15.79g | Protein 4.23g

Rice, Grains, and Pasta Recipe

Herby Chicken Rice

Prep time: 10 minutes | Cook time: 24 minutes | Serves: 4

Ingredients:

5-Ingredients:

4 chicken breasts, cut into thin strips

2 leeks, chopped

1 ½ cups basmati rice, rinsed

1 tbsp freshly chopped scallions

1 lemon, zested and juiced

Items from your pantry:

1 tbsp olive oil

Salt and freshly ground black pepper to taste

1 tbsp butter

1 yellow onion, diced

2 garlic cloves, minced

½ cup white wine

1 cup chicken broth

1 tsp dried dill

1 tsp dried parsley

Instructions

1. Select Sear/Sauté and adjust to Medium-High. Press Start to preheat the pot for 5 minutes.
2. Heat the olive oil in the inner pot, season the chicken with salt and black pepper, and brown in the oil on all sides, 5 minutes. Transfer to a plate and set aside.
3. Add the butter to the pot and allow melting. Sauté the leeks and onion until softened, 3 minutes. Mix in the garlic and cook until fragrant, 30 seconds.
4. Stir in the rice, white wine, chicken broth, chicken, salt, and black pepper.
5. Cover with the Pressure Lid and lock the vent to Seal. Select Pressure; adjust to High and the cook time to 5 minutes. Press Start to begin cooking.
6. After cooking, allow the pot to sit uncovered for 10 minutes, perform a quick pressure release, and open the lid.
7. Pour on the dill, parsley, scallions, lemon zest, and lemon juice. Fluff the rice while you stir until well mixed.
8. Dish the rice and serve warm.

Nutrition Facts per Serving

Calories 877 | Fats 49.23g | Carbs 30.71g | Net Carbs 20.43g | Protein 87.99g

Thai Teriyaki Rice

Prep time: 15 minutes | Cook time: 24 minutes | Serves: 4

Ingredients:

4-Ingredients:

1 large red bell pepper, deseeded and chopped

1 cup jasmine rice, rinsed

Items from your pantry:

1 tbsp sesame oil

1 large red onion, finely chopped

1 garlic clove, minced

1 cup chicken broth

¾ cup teriyaki sauce

1 cup fresh snow peas

1 tbsp sesame seeds, for garnishing

Instructions

1. Select Sear/Sauté and adjust to Medium-High. Press Start to preheat the pot for 5 minutes.
2. Heat the sesame oil in the inner pot and sauté the bell pepper and onion until softened, 5 minutes. Stir in the garlic and cook until fragrant, 30 seconds.
3. Mix in the rice, chicken broth, and teriyaki sauce.
4. Cover with the Pressure Lid and lock the vent to Seal. Select Pressure; adjust to High and the cook time to 5 minutes. Press Start to begin cooking.
5. After cooking, allow the pot to sit uncovered for 10 minutes, perform a quick pressure release, and open the lid.
6. Mix in the snow peas and set the pot in Warm mode until the peas warm through, 3 minutes.
7. Dish the rice, garnish with sesame seeds, and serve warm.

Nutrition Facts per Serving

Calories 200 | Fats 11.18g | Carbs 24.93g | Net Carbs 18.23g | Protein 9.07g

Italian Beef Cheesy Rice

Prep time: 15 minutes | Cook time: 22 minutes | Serves: 4

Ingredients:

5-Ingredients:

1 lb. ground beef

1 yellow bell pepper, deseeded and diced

1 cup basmati rice, rinsed

2 cups chopped kale

½ cup shredded Mexican cheese blend

Items from your pantry:

1 tbsp olive oil

Salt and freshly ground black pepper to taste

1 yellow onion, diced

2 garlic cloves, minced

1 tbsp Italian seasoning

1 cup beef broth

¼ cup tomato sauce

Instructions

1. Select Sear/Sauté and adjust to Medium-High. Press Start to preheat the pot for 5 minutes.
2. Heat the olive oil in the inner pot and cook the beef until brown, 5 minutes. Season with salt and black pepper, stir, and break the lumps that form.
3. Stir in the onion, bell pepper, garlic, and cook until the vegetables soften and the garlic fragrant, 30 seconds.
4. Mix in the rice, Italian seasoning, cook for 1 minute, and mix in the beef broth and tomato sauce.
5. Cover with the Pressure Lid and lock the vent to Seal. Select Pressure; adjust to High and the cook time to 5 minutes. Press Start.
6. After cooking, allow the pot to sit uncovered for 10 minutes, perform a quick pressure release, and open the lid.
7. Select Sear/Sauté and adjust to Medium.
8. Stir in the cheese and cook until melted.
9. Dish the rice onto serving plates and serve warm.

Nutrition Facts per Serving

Calories 558 | Fats 21.93g | Carbs 47.54g | Net Carbs 43.44g | Protein 40.1g

Corn & Scallion Oatmeal

Prep time: 10 minutes | Cook time: 13 minutes | Serves: 4

Ingredients:

5-Ingredients:

1 cup old fashioned rolled oats

1 cup fresh corn kernels

4 scallions, sliced and divided

½ tsp black sesame seeds for garnishing

Items from your pantry:

2 cups vegetable broth

2 tbsp soy sauce

1 tsp hot sauce

Salt and freshly ground black pepper to taste

Instructions

1. In the inner pot, mix the vegetable broth, soy sauce, hot sauce, oats, corn, and half of the scallions.
2. Cover with the Pressure Lid and lock the vent to Seal. Select Pressure; adjust to High and the cook time to 3 minutes. Press Start.
3. After cooking, perform a natural pressure release for 10 minutes, then a quick pressure release, and open the lid.
4. Stir and season the oatmeal with salt and black pepper.
5. Dish the food into serving bowls and garnish with the remaining scallions and sesame seeds.

Nutrition Facts per Serving

Calories 137 | Fats 4.63g | Carbs 25.44g | Net Carbs 20.24g | Protein 8.39g

Barley-Spinach Bowl

Prep time: 15 minutes | Cook time: 22 minutes | Serves: 4

Ingredients:

5-Ingredients:

1 cup pearl barley

4 oz baby spinach, chopped

4 oz ham, chopped

2 scallions, chopped for garnishing

Items from your pantry:

1 tbsp olive oil

¼ cup finely chopped red onion

½ cup water

1 ½ cups chicken broth

Salt and freshly ground black pepper to taste

¼ tsp red chili flakes

Instructions

1. Select Sear/Sauté and adjust to Medium-High. Press Start to preheat the pot for 5 minutes.
2. Heat the olive oil in the inner pot and sauté the barley and onion until fragrant, 4 minutes.
3. Mix in the water, chicken broth, salt, and black pepper.
4. Cover with the Pressure Lid and lock the vent to Seal. Select Pressure; adjust to High and the cook time to 18 minutes. Press Start to begin cooking.
5. After cooking, perform a quick pressure release, and open the lid.
6. Select Sear/Sauté and adjust to Medium-High. Press Start.
7. Stir in the spinach and ham; cook until the spinach wilts and adjust the taste with salt and black pepper.
8. Dish the food, garnish with the scallions and red chili flakes. Serve warm.

Nutrition Facts per Serving

Calories 423 | Fats 14.29g | Carbs 41.29g | Net Carbs 32.69g | Protein 32.59g

Raisins Buckwheat Pilaf

Prep time: 15 minutes | Cook time: 21 minutes | Serves: 4

Ingredients:

5-Ingredients:

1 medium red bell pepper, deseeded and diced

½ cup yellow lentils

1 cup roasted buckwheat groats

½ cup golden raisins

½ cup toasted walnuts

Items from your pantry:

1 tbsp olive oil

4 garlic cloves, minced

1 ¼ cups chicken broth

Salt and freshly ground black pepper to taste

¾ tsp dried thyme

Instructions

1. Select Sear/Sauté and adjust to Medium-High. Press Start to preheat the pot for 5 minutes.

2. Heat the olive oil in the inner pot and sauté the bell pepper until softened, 4 minutes. Stir in the garlic and cook until fragrant, 30 seconds.

3. Mix in the lentils, buckwheat, raisins, chicken broth, salt, black pepper, and thyme.

4. Cover with the Pressure Lid and lock the vent to Seal. Select Pressure; adjust to High and the cook time to 6 minutes. Press Start.

5. After cooking, perform a natural pressure release for 10 minutes, then a quick pressure release, and open the lid.

6. Stir in the walnuts and adjust the taste with salt and black pepper.

7. Dish the food into serving bowls and serve warm.

Nutrition Facts per Serving

Calories 225 | Fats 10.57g | Carbs 31.44g | Net Carbs 27.94g | Protein 5.5g

Creole-Style Grits & Shrimp

Prep time: 15 minutes | Cook time: 38 minutes | Serves: 4

Ingredients:

5-Ingredients:

6 oz andouille sausage, diced

1 (8 oz) canned diced tomatoes

1 cup corn grits

1 lb. jumbo shrimp, peeled and deveined

1/3 cup heavy cream

Items from your pantry:

1 tbsp olive oil

1 yellow onion, diced

2 garlic cloves, minced

1 cup white wine

1 tsp cayenne pepper or to taste

1 tbsp Creole seasoning

1 cup whole milk

1 cup chicken broth

1 tbsp butter

1 tbsp dried parsley

Instructions

1. Select Sear/Sauté and adjust to Medium-High. Press Start to preheat the pot for 5 minutes.

2. Heat the olive oil in the inner pot and brown the sausage on all sides, 5 minutes.

3. Stir in the onion, garlic, and cook until fragrant and softened, 3 minutes.

4. Mix in the white wine, allow reduction by one-third, 3 minutes. Add the tomatoes, cayenne peppers, and Creole seasoning.

5. While beginning to boil, in a large ramekin bowl, mix the grits, milk, and chicken broth. Fix the Reversible Rack over the sauce in the inner pot and place the grits bowl on top.

6. Cover with the Pressure Lid and lock the vent to Seal. Select Pressure; adjust to High and the cook time to 10 minutes. Press Start.

7. After cooking, perform a natural pressure release for 10 minutes, then a quick pressure release, and open the lid.

8. Remove the grits bowl and mix in the butter. Set aside for serving.

9. Remove the rack and select Sear/Sauté mode. Press Start to continue cooking the sauce.

10. Stir in the parsley and shrimp. Cook until the shrimp is pink, 5 minutes and stir in the heavy cream. Cook for 2 minutes.

11. Dish the grits into serving bowls and top with the shrimp and sauce. Serve warm.

Nutrition Facts per Serving

Calories 555 | Fats 23.58g | Carbs 48.99g | Net Carbs 43.09g | Protein 39.42g

Watercress Tagliatelle with Smoked Salmon

Prep time: 15 minutes | Cook time: 10 minutes | Serves: 4

Ingredients:

3-Ingredients:

16 oz green tagliatelle

1 cup watercress leaves + more to garnish

2 oz smoked salmon, cut into thin strips

Items from your pantry:

1 tbsp olive oil

2 garlic cloves, minced

Salt and freshly ground black pepper to taste

Instructions

1. In the inner pot, add the pasta, 4 cups of water, and salt.
2. Cover with the Pressure Lid and lock the vent to Seal. Select Pressure; adjust to High and the cook time to 3 minutes. Press Start.
3. After cooking, perform a quick pressure release, and open the lid. Drain the pasta through a colander and set aside. Clean the inner pot and return the pot to the base.
4. Select Sear/Sauté and adjust to Medium-High. Press Start to preheat the pot for 5 minutes.
5. Heat the olive oil in the inner pot and sauté the garlic until fragrant, 30 seconds.
6. Stir in the watercress and salmon; cook for 1 minute. Mix in the tagliatelle using tongs and season with salt and black pepper.
7. Dish the food onto serving plates, garnish with some watercress leaves, and serve warm.

Nutrition Facts per Serving

Calories 80 | Fats 4.55g | Carbs 5.52g | Net Carbs 1.22g | Protein 5.71g

Creamy Bucatini with Chicken

Prep time: 15 minutes | Cook time: 17 minutes | Serves: 4

Ingredients:

5-Ingredients:

1 ½ cups dried bucatini

4 chicken breasts, cut into 1-inch cubes

¼ cup heavy cream

14 cup frozen peas

2 tbsp freshly chopped parsley to garnish

Items from your pantry:

1 tbsp olive oil

Salt and freshly ground black pepper to taste

4 tbsp white wine

Instructions

1. In the inner pot, add the pasta, 4 cups of water, and salt.
2. Cover with the Pressure Lid and lock the vent to Seal. Select Pressure; adjust to High and the cook time to 3 minutes. Press Start.
3. After cooking, perform a quick pressure release, and open the lid. Drain the pasta through a colander and set aside. Clean the inner pot and return the pot to the base.
4. Select Sear/Sauté and adjust to Medium-High. Press Start to preheat the pot for 5 minutes.
5. Heat the olive oil in the inner pot, season the chicken with salt, black pepper, and cook in the oil until golden brown on all sides, 6 to 8 minutes.
6. Pour in the white wine, cook for 1 minute, and stir in the heavy cream. Cook some more for 1 minute.
7. Stir in the peas, bucatini, and season with salt and pepper. Stir until well coated in the sauce.
8. Dish the food and garnish with the parsley. Serve warm.

Nutrition Facts per Serving

Calories 846 | Fats 34.61g | Carbs 58.03g | Net Carbs 39.53g | Protein 75.16g

Spaghetti in Saffron Sauce

Prep time: 15 minutes | Cook time: 13 minutes | Serves: 4

Ingredients:

4-Ingredients:

16 oz spaghetti

2 cups heavy cream

Items from your pantry:

2 tbsp butter

1 tbsp olive oil

1 medium brown onion, chopped

2 garlic cloves, minced

1 egg yolk

½ lemon, juiced

2 tsp corn flour

A pinch saffron powder

Salt and freshly ground black pepper to taste

Instructions

1. In the inner pot, add the spaghetti, 4 cups of water, and salt.
2. Cover with the Pressure Lid and lock the vent to Seal. Select Pressure; adjust to High and the cook time to 3 minutes. Press Start.
3. After cooking, perform a quick pressure release, and open the lid. Drain the pasta through a colander and set aside. Clean the inner pot and return the pot to the base.
4. Select Sear/Sauté and adjust to Medium-High. Press Start to preheat the pot for 5 minutes.
5. Heat the butter and olive in the inner pot and sauté the onion until softened, 3 minutes. Mix in the garlic and cook until fragrant, 30 seconds.
6. Whisk in the corn flour and cook for 1 minute. After, gradually whisk in the heavy cream until a smooth mixture is attained and then, vigorously whisk in the egg yolk and saffron to prevent the egg from cooking into lumps.
7. Stir in the lemon juice, salt, black pepper, and spaghetti until well mixed.
8. Dish the food onto serving plates and serve warm.

Nutrition Facts per Serving

Calories 461 | Fats 33.17g | Carbs 36.25g | Net Carbs 30.55g | Protein 8.51g

Lightning Source UK Ltd.
Milton Keynes UK
UKHW051022281021
392990UK00007B/439